EVIL INVENTIONS

Nick Arnold and Tony De Saulles

■SCHOLASTIC

www.scholastic.co.uk

Scholastic Children's Books,
Euston House, 24 Eversholt Street,
London NW1 1DB, UK

A division of Scholastic Ltd
London ~ New York ~ Toronto ~ Sydney ~ Auckland
Mexico City ~ New Delhi ~ Hong Kong

First published in the UK by Scholastic Ltd, 2007
This revised and updated edition published by Scholastic Ltd, 2014

Text copyright © Nick Arnold, 2007, 2014
Illustrations copyright © Tony De Saulles, 2007, 2014
Index by Caroline Hamilton

ISBN 978 1407 14292 0

Printed and bound by CPI Group (UK) Ltd, Croydon, CR0 4YY

2 4 6 8 10 9 7 5 3 1

CONTENTS

Nick Arnold has been writing stories and books since he was a youngster, but never dreamt he'd find fame writing about Evil Inventions. His research involved trying on the goofy gerbil fun shirt and he enjoyed every minute of it.

When he's not delving into Horrible Science, he spends his spare time eating pizza, riding his bike and thinking up corny jokes (though not all at the same time).

www.nickarnold-website.com

Tony De Saulles picked up his crayons when he was still in nappies and has been doodling ever since. He takes Horrible Science very seriously and even agreed to strap on a pair of wheelie wonder wheels and whizz down a steep hill. Fortunately, he's made a full recovery. When he's not out with his sketchpad, Tony likes to write poetry and play squash, though he hasn't written any poetry about squash yet.

www.tonydesaulles.co.uk

INTRODUCTION

Have you ever dreamt up a new machine or a new way of doing something? If so you've hit on an invention – maybe it was something like...

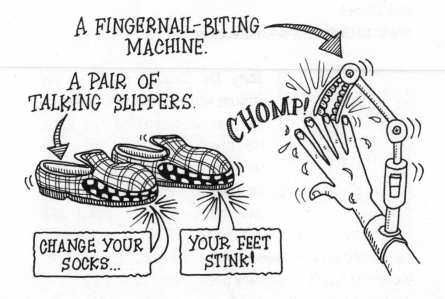

A FINGERNAIL-BITING MACHINE.

A PAIR OF TALKING SLIPPERS.

CHOMP!

CHANGE YOUR SOCKS...

YOUR FEET STINK!

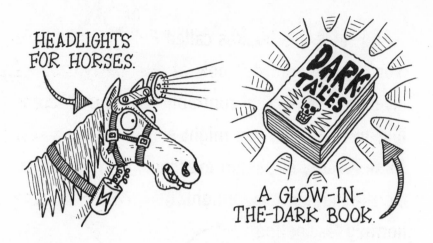

HEADLIGHTS FOR HORSES.

DARK TALES

A GLOW-IN-THE-DARK BOOK.

Well, in this book we'll be exploring the weird, wacky world of inventions — including the incredibly exciting and incredibly idiotic thingies that people dream up.

An urgent note from the author
Help! There are thousands and THOUSANDS of inventions and I can't fit them all into this book. Oh well, I'll just have to tell you about a few important inventions — plus the stunningly silly ones of course!

And since this book is called *Evil Inventions* we won't be scared to look at the nasty side of inventing – the cruel contraptions and murderous machines. In fact you might end up wondering if some inventions should ever have been invented. Or then again, you might find evil inventions horribly fascinating...

HOW TO BE AN INCREDIBLE INVENTOR

So could YOU dream up an incredible invention and make massive mounds of money and become ridiculously famous? It's time to learn the necessary know-how and check out your chances of success…

THE HORRIBLE SCIENCE INVENTORS' TRAINING COURSE

LESSON 1 Have you got the urge to invent?

Anyone can be an inventor as long as they want to invent something… Of course inventors come in all shapes and sizes. But our experts in this book,

Professor Z and Nora Nasty are *evil* inventors. They'll be taking a break from building evil inventions and trying to take over the world to tell us about the science behind inventions…

But most inventors are nice people, and some tend to wear crumpled clothes, odd socks and a vacant expression.

Inventors do their job for lots of reasons. Some enjoy dreaming up incredible ideas. Some seek to make life better for everyone. And others just want fame and…

HUGE WADS OF MONEY!

But before you can earn a penny there's something you just have to do…

LESSON 2 Have a bright idea!

Anyone can have a bright idea. Well, maybe not *anyone*. I don't suppose your pet dog has too many bright ideas…

But if your idea is going to change the world it's got to be an invention people want so much that they'll actually *pay* for it...

No, Professor Z – I was thinking more in terms of earmuffs. Just look at this...

THE SECRET DIARY OF CHESTER GREENWOOD

Maine, USA, 1873

My birthday

Dear Diary
My ears have ruined my life! Today's my birthday, and I got a pair of ice skates. WOW! I thought. I just couldn't wait to try them out on the pond. The weather was snowy and freezing - just right for skating. But it was too cold for my ugly elephant flappers! Everyone laughs at the way my ears turn from red to purple to white in the cold. Today they let me down BIG TIME!

SHIVER!

My cold ears hurt so much I couldn't even skate! ➞

Next day

Dear Diary
Today I got smart - well I tried - I decided to keep my ears warm by wrapping a scarf around them. Well, it seemed like a good idea at the time. But it's real hard to skate with an itchy rug of a scarf wound around your face. The wool made my poor ears itch so much that I stopped skating to scratch them. And when I took off the scarf I felt as if the cold was chewing my head-flappers off.

Next day

Dear Diary
My gran's worth her weight in gold - but it was my idea. I got two wire loops and Gran sewed velvet on one side of each loop and beaver fur on the outside. I put the loops over my ears and they worked!!! I skated for ages without my ears turning bright red. It was GREAT!!!

Chilly Chester had spotted a need – to stop his cold ears dropping off – and figured out an invention to meet that need. And the story doesn't end there. Chester added a piece of wire that fitted over his head and kept the earmuffs in place. At last, in 1877, he felt his design was ready to sell to the public. Here's what he said...

I BELIEVE PERFECTION HAS BEEN REACHED!

Chester was soon up to his ears in earmuff orders. And today in Chester's hometown, 21 December is celebrated with a parade and a "who's got the coldest ears?" contest.

If you invent something brilliant you don't want a gang of evil inventors pinching your idea and pretending they came up with it first. So you need to get your invention patented. A patent means that you're the only person who can make or sell your invention. A patent contains a description of the invention, how it works and what's new about it. And if that sounds like a lot of work, you're right – it is. A patent costs lots of money and may take years to get.

IN THE MEANTIME IT'S A GOOD IDEA TO KEEP YOUR INVENTION A SECRET...

SO I WON'T STEAL IT!

LESSON 3 Keep a notebook ... and get quick on the draw!

Budding inventors need a notebook for their brilliant brainwaves – if you don't have notebook, you could always use a school book or even a sheet of toilet paper. Of course it helps if you can draw your idea too. Oh yes, and it does help if you're the sort of person who has ten brilliant brainwaves before breakfast. A bit like this man...

INCREDIBLE INVENTOR FILES

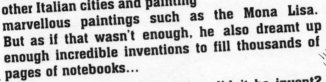

NAME: Leonardo da Vinci (1452–1519)

NATIONALITY: Italian

CLAIM TO FAME: Many experts think Leo was the greatest artist ever. He spent much of his life living in Milan and other Italian cities and painting marvellous paintings such as the Mona Lisa. But as if that wasn't enough, he also dreamt up enough incredible inventions to fill thousands of pages of notebooks...

INCREDIBLE INVENTIONS: What didn't he invent? Leo came up with designs for submarines and helicopters and flying machines and diving suits and cars driven by springs and a kind of robot man in armour. And he thought up these incredible ideas hundreds of years before anyone else.

DREADFUL DETAILS: Leo was the original horrible scientist. He cut up dead bodies in order to improve his drawing skills and he enjoyed playing revolting practical jokes such as filling a bull's guts with air during a party.

DON'T MENTION: Leo never built most of his inventions and they were forgotten after his death. It's said he got an assistant to test his flying machine but it crashed.

AWFUL END: The French king allowed the artist to live in one of his castles, and that's where he died. Three hundred years later Leo's bones were dug up and lost when his tomb was repaired. It's said local kids used Leo's bones as skittles.

Here's a peek at one of Leo's notebooks, complete with some of his inventions.[1]

1 OK this is a forgery by our equally talented Horrible Science artist. The real notebooks were written in mirror-writing and we couldn't read a word of them.

Modern experts agree that the flying machine and helicopter didn't have enough power to fly but in 2000, skydiver Adrian Nicholas tested the parachute in South Africa.

"Mr da Vinci, maybe you were right!" he yelled as he dropped from a hot-air balloon. In fact the parachute worked fine, but the sensible skydiver switched to a modern parachute before landing.

Lesson 4 Don't forget to experiment!

It's useful to grasp the science behind your invention. And, as we'll be finding out, most modern inventions have been based on scientific discoveries.

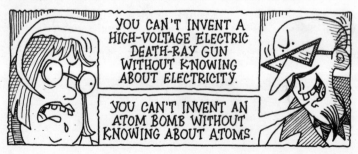

YOU CAN'T INVENT A HIGH-VOLTAGE ELECTRIC DEATH-RAY GUN WITHOUT KNOWING ABOUT ELECTRICITY.

YOU CAN'T INVENT AN ATOM BOMB WITHOUT KNOWING ABOUT ATOMS.

Anyway, back to experiments... Once you've built your glow-in-the-dark nail-biting machine, you'll need to test it in a scientific fashion to make sure it works.

A TERRIBLE TEST YOU SHOULDN'T TRY

In 1859 US chemist Robert Chesebrough (1837–1933) tested a greasy gunk that had been found stuck to oil drills. The slimy substance was called petroleum jelly, and oil workers believed that it speeded up healing. Crazy Chesebrough tested the substance in a sickening way. He CUT and BURNT his own body and splatted the goo over it. The wounds healed. Robert called the substance "Vaseline" and advertised it by burning and cutting his body some more and proudly showing off his healthy healing wounds.

Vaseline proved ideal for greasing machinery and shifting stains too, and Robert Chesebrough lived to a ripe and rich old age. He said his secret was a daily dose of Vaseline – he used to EAT it!

HORRIBLE HEALTH WARNING!

Vaseline actually aided healing by sealing wounds from germs — but a clean bandage is just as good. As for eating Vaseline, don't even think about it! If you must scoff jelly, stick to jelly babies!

I BITE THE HEADS OFF MINE!

And here's another test you should NEVER try. Can you believe it – in 1929 a young surgeon tested an invention idea by sticking a tube ... into his OWN HEART?! Here's how the nurse who helped him might have remembered the terrible test...

Werner Forssmann's heart-tube test

By his nurse, Eva

Everyone at Berlin City Hospital knew about Werner Forssmann and his odd habits. He was a bit of a loner, and kept himself to himself. And he was always reading vets' magazines about how to take blood from animals through rubber tubes. Vets' magazines? He was supposed to be treating humans not animals!

I suppose that's where he got his idea for a heart tube.

"It will be quite safe, Eva," he promised. "I simply want you to cut open one of my veins and push in a rubber tube. I will guide it to my heart. If the test works, my new invention will make it possible to send drugs to the heart safely."

EH?

Werner was excited. His eyes were bright in his pale face, but I wasn't so sure.

"It doesn't sound safe to me," I worried.

"It is, I promise," said Werner. "I have tested it on a corpse and it didn't complain once!"

On the day of our experiment I still had my doubts, but I'm a nurse – I'm trained to do what I'm told.

So I cut open the vein in Werner's arm and pushed the tube in. Then I held a mirror to help Werner see an X-ray screen as he pushed the tube higher.

The screen showed the tube as a dark shadow snaking up inside Werner's veins and creeping towards his heart as he pushed it further and further into his body.

I couldn't bear to watch. I could scarcely breathe. This is madness, I thought wildly – but it was too late.

At last Werner stopped with a gasp. Beads of sweat stood out on his brow.

"I can feel it in my heart," he whispered.

And I can see it, I thought, glancing nervously at the X-ray screen.

"I must tell the other doctors," gasped Werner triumphantly.

"But wait…" I began.

I was too late. Werner had already left the X-ray room with one end of the tube in his heart and the other end trailing from his arm. I could hear him painfully dragging himself up two flights of stairs. Of course I offered to help but he wouldn't hear of it. Like a typical surgeon – he wanted to do it all by himself. I heard later that he saw another doctor who didn't believe him. Together they examined the image on another X-ray screen and took photos.

A few minutes later Werner was back. He looked paler than ever now. His lips were tight with pain.

"I don't feel quite so well," he said weakly. "Perhaps I should lie down."

I bit my lip as I helped him to pull the tube gently from his arm. I really wanted to say "You silly man – of course you don't feel well! Who can feel well after climbing two flights of stairs with a tube in their heart?"

But we nurses can't talk to surgeons like that, and so I said nothing until the job was done and the tube was out.

"Thank you," gasped Werner – his face cold and clammy with sweat. "Thank you again ... from the bottom of my heart."

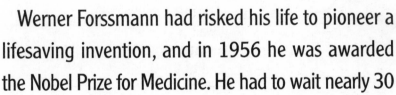

Werner Forssmann had risked his life to pioneer a lifesaving invention, and in 1956 he was awarded the Nobel Prize for Medicine. He had to wait nearly 30 years for the prize but at least he didn't wait in "vein".

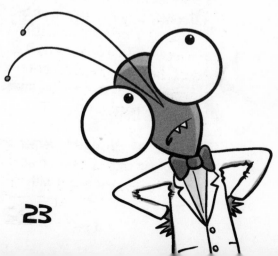

Lesson 5 Get an organization behind you

Every successful inventor needs money. So it helps to have…

YOUR VERY OWN FACTORY

FILTHY RICH PARENTS

A RIDICULOUSLY RICH BUSINESS PARTNER

And it also helps to have an understanding family who don't mind if you shut yourself in the garden shed for months.

Of course you might want to recruit a team of friends to help you. This is what top US inventor Thomas Edison (1847–1931) did. He built an invention "factory" at Menlo Park, USA. The factory had lots of tools and bits and pieces to build inventions with. Edison spent his life thinking up inventions and his talented team made them.

This approach worked. Edison invented an early form of cinema, light bulb, electrical supply, sound recording and in all he came up with 1,089 inventions.

Edison was a genuine genius who came up with loads more inventions than anyone else. But every inventor makes mistakes and Edison was no exception. For example, there's the

EDISON HAVING A BRIGHT IDEA!

embarrassing fact that few people got the chance to see his films because you had to take turns to peer through the eyepiece of a weird machine, or that his light bulb and electricity system needed huge improvements to work properly. Or the fact that Edison didn't understand why anyone wanted to listen to recorded music. Oh yes, and let's not mention the great man's horrible habit of spitting on the floor. Edison claimed you had more chance of hitting the floor than a hitting a bowl. Maybe – but it's gross, especially when you hit someone's shoes! That's why directed dribbling isn't part of your training course!

Today the support of a big organization is even more important for inventors than it was in Edison's day. It costs loads of money to develop and test new ideas. And that's why modern inventors often work for big companies.

Lesson 6 Don't give up hope ... EVER!

The sad fact is that even when carefully tested and backed with lorry-loads of lolly, most inventions fail. People don't like them and they won't buy them. Sometimes they're too expensive to make.

BET YOU NEVER KNEW!

In the 1900s US inventor Joseph Karwowski spent a fortune encasing dead bodies in glass. It was harder than you think because if the glass was hot enough to melt, the body would be cooked. At last he managed to make moulds in the shape of the body and created them in glass. But the inventor's glass dreams shattered because people weren't too keen on having their dear departed dead relatives staring at them across the breakfast table. Perhaps he should have made perished pet paperweights instead?

Of course many inventions fail in tests (a bit like children, I guess). Thomas Edison once said:

YOU'VE GOT TO MAKE THE DARN THING WORK ... I HAVE FAILED MY WAY TO SUCCESS.

DON'T SPIT IN MY NICE CLEAN BOOK!

SSSPURP!

What Edison meant was that an inventor can learn from their mistakes and improve their inventions until they work properly. Dare you quote this to your teacher next time you fail a science test?

Certainly we at the Horrible Science Inventors' Training Course believe you shouldn't give up. And here's a true story that might inspire you to struggle on…

THE INCREDIBLE RUBBER MAN

Back in the 1830s, inventors had a sickeningly sticky problem. Rubber was made from gooey sap that oozed from rubber trees when you cut them. But before rubber could be made into boots, some way had to be found to stop it from melting in hot weather and cracking in the cold. In the USA, one man struggled to find the answer. His name was Charles Goodyear...

Charles was so crazy about rubber that he wore a rubber hat and a rubber tie and had his portrait painted on rubber. And (I know you won't believe this bit) he even wrote his life story in a rubber book with rubber pages!

BLAST, A SPELLING MISTAKE - WHERE'S MY RUBBER?

If he'd written a rubber diary, it might have looked like this...

WARNING TO SENSITIVE READERS!

This story is extremely sad and you may feel the urge to blubber about rubber. If affected DO NOT blow your nose on this book — it's NOT made of rubber and it won't wipe clean!

"MY "RUBBER" DIARY"
by Charles Goodyear

1834 ~ I've got a dream - to invent a new kind of rubber that doesn't melt or crack. But there's a problem. I've been thrown into jail because I didn't have enough cash to pay a $5 hotel bill. Oh well, a friend's given me a little money and Mrs Goodyear's lent me her rolling pin. So I'll carry on working in jail, and I bet this time next year I'll be rich!

1837 ~ These have been bad years for the Goodyears. I nearly poisoned myself with the gases from my experiments and we had to move because the smells upset the neighbours.
I figured that adding nitric acid to rubber would make it harder. I tried twice to make the new substance. Once my partner lost all his money and once I did. The rubber mailbags I was making for the US Government proved useless and rotten. Now I'm back in jail. But I won't give up my dream. I'll bounce back like a rubber ball and when I do I'll be rich - just you see!

1839 ~ Last night I made a great discovery! By accident I dropped a bit of rubber mixed with sulphur on Mrs G's stove.

It should have melted but it didn't. That little piece of rubber was blackened and yet by some miracle it had become stronger. Trembling from head to toe, I left the rubber outside my kitchen door in the cold. Would it crack? NO! This morning it was as bendy as ever. At last I've cracked the problem (but not the rubber!). At long last - Dame Fortune is smiling on me!

BEND!

1844 ~ All this time I've been testing my invention. My poor family have been homeless and we've had to live in an old factory and wear rubber shoes and eat off rubber plates. I've had to beg for food. During these terrible years, six of my dear little children have died and I had to sell everything we owned - even the children's books. But I've never sold my dream and now at long last my invention is ready to be made in a factory. And this time next year I'm going to be rich...

I ALWAYS BOUNCE BACK!

31

Well, what do think happened? Charles Goodyear had wrecked his life to invent what he called "vulcanized rubber". He had to sleep in sheds and wade through snow and go hungry. He became so crippled by suffering and hardship that he had to walk on crutches. Then other inventors stole his ideas.

By 1860 the multi-million dollar rubber industry was booming but no one even said "thank you" to the inspired inventor who had made it happen. Charles Goodyear said he didn't care for money, and only wanted to help others. But he never became rich and he died a forgotten man.

We asked Professor Z to explain Goodyear's discovery...

RUBBER IS A POLYMER. THAT MEANS IT'S MADE FROM CHAINS OF MOLECULES — GROUPS OF ATOMS LINKED TOGETHER.

WHEN I HEAT RUBBER AND SULPHUR, THE SULPHUR MOLECULES LINK THE RUBBER MOLECULES LIKE A NET. THIS STRONGER SUBSTANCE IS VULCANIZED RUBBER.

USEFUL THINGS, NETS — HEH HEH!

HUH?

Well, that's the Horrible Science Inventors' Training Course over — and now for some bad news.

After all your hard work, your invention might still be a flop. According to Art Fry, American inventor of the Post-it note, out of 5,000 ideas only one ever makes it to the shops.

We're going to take a commercial break now for some inventions that didn't quite make it...

AWFUL ADVERTISEMENTS 1

A QUICK NOTE FROM THE AUTHOR
All the inventions in our awful adverts were patented but either they never went on sale or they never caught on. As far as I know none of them are on sale today.

THE DOGGIE WATCH

Here's a timepiece your pet really can count on! It's the world's first watch ... for dogs!
Your dog will never ask you the time again or want to go walkies too early! This American 1991 canine chronometer* is a masterpiece of hound horology!** It's set to doggie-time (one year counts as seven) so your dog knows how fast its life is slipping away!

BLAST, I'M LATE!

*Posh word for clock.
**Art of clock making.

SAY GOODBYE TO POOPING PETS!

Badog's troubles are over with the new PET POTTY. You simply train your pet to climb up the beautiful staircase and sit on the cunningly designed toilet trapdoor.

D'YOU MIND?

PLOP!

After your pet has performed, the fun really starts! A high-tech sensor switches on the flushing system to clean the trapdoor tray and the trapdoor opens to drop the doo-doo down the loo. SPLOSH!

The small print - If your pet is a greedy guts they might be too heavy for the trapdoor and Badog might take a tumble into the toilet.

SPLASH OUT ON A POOCH PORTA-POTTY

Brighten Badog's day with this cool doggie designer fashion item! Simply strap the pooch porta-potty on your dog and away you go!

AHHHHH, THAT'S BETTER!

And now for the GOOD NEWS – this pooch porta-potty is made of rubber and you'll just LURVE washing it out so your pet can use it again and again!

GIDDY UP THERE!

Ever wanted to ride a horse but been scared to get on one?
Well, now you don't have to! Simply control your horse from a safe distance with this handy remote-control zapper (USA 1981)!

SUPER SADDLE PULLS THE REINS AND EVEN WHIPS DOBBIN WHEN HE'S BEEN A NAUGHTY NAG!

WHACK!

OUCH!

KEEP YOUR HOME CLEAN WITH A KITTY DUSTER!

No more dreary dusting! Simply put these high-fashion feline footsocks on Tiddles and enjoy watching her knock your priceless ornaments off the mantelpiece!

WHOOPS!

GIVE TIDDLES A TWEET TREAT!

Make your cat's suppertime fun with this new cat feeder!

COOL! A NEW HOME!

BIRD GETS TRAPPED INSIDE THE PIPE AND ENDS UP IN THE CAGE.

You train Tiddles to lift the cage door and grab a bite-sized birdie! Hours and hours of feline fun! Guaranteed to get rid of unwanted wildlife!

YUMMY!

GIVE THE DOG A LIFT!

Even the most playful dog needs a nap, but Badog can still meet new friends with this lovingly designed doggie mobile home! Thanks to this American 1994 invention you can even take your dog to a party – just so long as you don't mind the odd wee accident down your shirt!

ERK!

GOTTA DASH FOR THE PLANE?

This delightful doggie designer suitcase (USA 1998) means you'll never leave your pampered pooch at the check-in!

WHAT A SPECTACLE!

Now your chickens can see in comfort with these trendy plastic eye-protectors. They're something to crow about!

The small print - In 1902 US inventor Andrew Jackson came up with the eyeglasses to stop horrible hens pecking out your favourite fowl's eyeballs. (Chickens sometimes do this when they're stressed.)

GET SOME POOCH PROTECTION!

OOER!

GET IN THE CAR, BADOG!

CHOMP! GUZZLE!

| The doggie bumper (USA 1977) stops your hound harming himself in a car crash (now he'll just bounce around instead). | Doggie ear-lifters (USA 1980) keep Badog's long ears away from his doggy dinner. |

We'll be inspecting more awful adverts later but now it's time for a high-speed time tour of inventions…

A TERRIFYING TIME TOUR

Welcome to the Terrifying Time Tour and who better to guide us than our very own evil inventors – plus their dog, of course!

... SOME BRIGHT SPARK!

Over 790,000 years ago: Someone discovers how to use fire. This vital discovery allows people to cook mammoth steaks. Later on, fire makes it possible to make pottery and work metals, and that's just for starters. No one knows who discovered fire...

5000 BC, Egypt and China: People paddle boats and rafts. Egyptian boats have sails before 3000 BC.

3500 BC, Iraq: The wheel makes it easier to move heavy loads and heavy people. Wheels later prove handy for windmills and other machines. Once again no one knows who came up with this "wheelie" good idea...

...BUT JUST IMAGINE IF THEY HADN'T!

287–212 BC, Sicily: Greek genius Archimedes is one of the first-known inventors. Awesome Archie develops ideas about levers and pulleys. When the Romans attack his city, Archie devises wicked weapons such as "the claw" – a crane with a giant lever and pulley that tips ships over. But these incredible inventions couldn't keep the Romans away and when they capture the city, a soldier stabs Archie to death.

868, China: Books are printed using blocks of carved wood. In the 1040s Bi Sheng invents type based on Chinese words. This can be used for more than one book.

1044: Chinese inventors make gunpowder. The explosive breakthrough leads to deadly destructive weapons such as cannon, hand grenades and bombs. At least it makes lovely fireworks too.

1450s: Johannes Gutenberg (c.1395–1468) develops printing in Europe. Printing gives people the chance to buy cheaper books and pick up new ideas and knowledge. It also made this book possible so it *must* have been a good thing...

1712: British inventor Thomas Newcomen invents an early steam engine. The steam engine powers trains and ships...

1783 France: The Montgolfier brothers invent the first balloon – they're puffed with success.

1830s: High-powered scientists such as British boffin Michael Faraday and American Joseph Henry get to grips with electrical machines. These powerful products power the world...

1880s Germany: The first car takes to the road ... and breaks down.

1888: German Heinrich Hertz (1857–1894) uses his electrical know-how to discover radio waves.

1903, USA: The Wright brothers fly their first plane. From now on it's plane sailing (until they crash).

1925, Britain: John Logie Baird invents TV. Eventually the world tunes in and parents and children stop talking to each other.

1930: US scientist Vannevar Bush builds an early computer. You can use it to solve sums but you can't play cool games on it.

1945: The atom bomb makes a huge impact – literally. For the first time humans have the power to destroy themselves.

1969: The first humans walk on the Moon, all thanks to the giant Saturn V rocket designed by German-born US inventor Wernher von Braun (1912–1977).

1975: Microchip computers appear. They're smaller, faster and more powerful than anything that went before them. In the next few years microchips change the world through mobile phones and DVD players and...

THE ROBOT COCKROACH

THE ANTI-SNORING BED

THE INTELLIGENT FRIDGE*

*These are all *real* inventions featured in this book...

Well, that's reached the present day, but hold on, I've forgotten to mention an important invention. In 1842 a blacksmith came up with a wonderful way of getting about on two wheels – can you guess what I'm talking about?

BARMY BIKES AND CRUEL CONTRAPTIONS

Bikes are brilliant – they're healthy and fun. You can get lots of fresh air as you pedal along and you can get lots of free rain on your head if you happen to get caught in a downpour. But who should we thank for this incredible invention?

Everything you need to know to be a bike expert in 30 seconds (just make sure you read this next bit really fast!)

1 Experts don't agree who invented the bike. Some say it was Scottish blacksmith Kirkpatrick Macmillan in 1842. Well, he *did* invent a bike – but not as we know it…

2 In fact lots of inventors helped to create the bike we know today. Some designed vital bike bits and others came up with new designs. A man named James Starley invented an especially barmy bike…

PENNY FARTHING (1870)

This mad machine was hard to get on to and even harder to get off unless you hit something and flew over the handlebars onto your head. But that didn't stop crazy cyclists riding on the tops of walls and racing down hills with their feet on the handlebars. Fortunately Starley's nephew, John, came up with something for cyclists who wanted to live to be old…

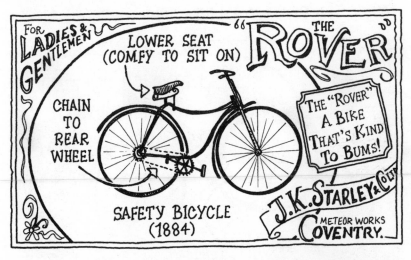

3 A modern bike (like yours) is amazing. It can pull the weight of two large adults on a trailer and turn 98% of your pedal power into movement energy (and that's more than most machines).

THREE BARMY BIKES

1 A "boneshaker" was a type of early bike built by French inventors Pierre and Ernest Michaux in the 1860s. The British called the bike the "boneshaker" because that's what it did to your bones when you rode on cobbles, but at least it didn't flop like these next two barmy bikes…

2 In 1984 a British inventor came up with a tricycle lawnmower for kids. The idea was that the kids would happily ride up and down the garden and cut the grass. The trouble is the wheels left nasty tracks on the lawn.

3 In 1988 an American inventor designed a sail-powered bike. The idea was great, but if the wind blew against you, you might get blown backwards. Or perhaps get blown in front of a passing lorry or wrapped around a passing traffic cop.

And talking about barmy bikes, here's the barmiest of the lot...

BARMY BIKE MANUAL (1889)

THANKS FOR BUYING ANTON OLESKIEWICZ'S
NEW HIGH-SPEED BIKE. IT'S DESIGNED TO
USE YOUR UPPER-BODY STRENGTH TO
PROVIDE EXTRA POWER!

How to ride:

1 Spend an hour putting on the harness that takes power from your upper body. Allow lots of time for this!

2 Attach yourself to the steel rod that lines up with the front of your chest. Check that the horizontal spring-loaded rod is linked up to the chain wheel under your saddle.

3 Pedal the bike as normal.

4 When you're going fast enough, throw your body violently backwards and forwards. The rods pass the energy through a series of chains to make the bike go faster.

5 Throw up.

6 Fall off your bike.

7 Get taken to hospital.

8 It's as simple as that!

All this really happened when the bike was tested in London. In fact, none of the cyclists could go faster than usual, but two fell off their bikes and several were sick. Could this be the only case in history of anyone getting travel sick on a bike?

BET YOU NEVER KNEW!

If you tried to steal Adolf Neubauer's bike in New York in 1900 you'd be taught a sharp lesson. As you tried to ride off, a spike would shoot up from the saddle and stab your backside. That could prove a sore point...

BRILLIANT BIKE BITS 'N' PIECES

All the bikes in this chapter have something in common...

THEY'VE GOT TWO WHEELS?

ISN'T THAT TWO THINGS IN COMMON?

No, no, no – I was about to say that all the bikes in this chapter include vital bits and pieces that are found in other inventions and here they are in Nora Nasty's bike…

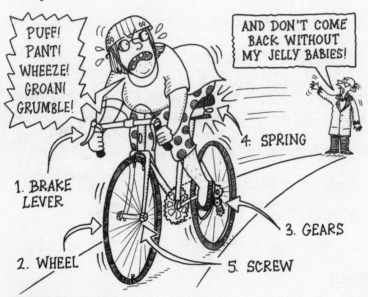

PUFF!
PANT!
WHEEZE!
GROAN!
GRUMBLE!

AND DON'T COME BACK WITHOUT MY JELLY BABIES!

4. SPRING

1. BRAKE LEVER

3. GEARS

2. WHEEL

5. SCREW

1 Brake lever

What it does: The brake lever allows Nora to control the brakes and stop the wheels turning. The idea behind a lever is it's easier to move something a longer distance with less force than to move something a shorter distance with more force. That's why it's harder to squeeze a brake lever closer to the handlebars.

Where else found: Scissors, nutcrackers, wheelbarrows, seesaws, tweezers and loads of other inventions. Ugh – don't look at this disgusting picture!

PLUCK!

2 Wheel

What it does: Wheels make things go round. So how come you knew that already? Well, I bet you never knew that a wheel is made up of lots of levers (they're the spokes)…

The shape of a wheel means that only part of it touches the ground at any one time. And this reduces the rubbing force known as friction that slows the bike down.

Where else found: Any wheeled transport. And bet you never knew that Thomas Edison invented a wheel turned by *sound*. The sound made a thin piece of metal called a diaphragm (dia-fram) vibrate (wobble) and the energy turned the wheel. It's a must for any loud-mouthed teacher!

3 Gears

What they do: Gears come in many sizes but they all pass on movement energy using their teeth.

GEAR WHEELS

PERFECT TEETH

WONKY TEETH

Where else found: Inventions such as car gears, clocks, corkscrews and tin openers – anywhere where a force needs to move a wheel. Oddly enough, modern tin openers weren't invented until 1920 – that's over ONE HUNDRED years *after* tinned food. Before then people had to open tins with a hammer, and US Civil War soldiers shot them open with guns.

4 Springs

What they do: Springs soak up energy and keep things in place. As Nora pedals, seat springs soak up the downward force of her backside.

Where else found: Springs store energy in clockwork machines. There are springs in staplers, toasters, mattresses, mousetraps and comfy chairs. (Just DON'T leave a mousetrap on your teacher's comfy chair or they might make a spring at you!) And then there are the very silly spring inventions...

One Victorian inventor devised a powerful spring-powered mousetrap that splattered the mouse on the ceiling. And I bet that wasn't a mice way to goo.

In 1994 a US inventor invented a wig-flipping machine and here it is…

At the touch of a button the wig dances up and down on your head. Hours of fun and laughter guaranteed I'm sure!

5 Screws

What they do: Screws are designed to fasten things together or control the position of objects.

Some screws can be turned in order to drill through an object.

Where else found: Screws are found in er ... screws, nuts, bolts and bottle tops. They're *supposed* to make opening the bottle *less* effort!

GRRRRR!

NUTTY PROFESSOR (WITH A SCREW LOOSE)

NOT THESE NUTS!

BiG NUTS

TRAGIC!

GRR — I'LL SHOW YOU SOME REALLY EVIL MACHINES WITH WHEELS AND LEVERS AND SCREWS!

PROFESSOR Z'S TOP FIVE EVIL INVENTIONS

I'm getting bored of all these goody-goody inventions. Read on and I promise you a truly painful experience — HEH HEH!

5 THE PANJANDRUM (BRITAIN 1944)
EVIL RATING — What goes around comes around! I love testing this giant rocket-powered wheel on holiday — it's sure to scare everyone else off the beach so I can have it all to myself.

VOOSH!

CAN I HAVE AN ICE CREAM, DAD?

The panjandrum was designed for attacking enemy beaches, but in tests the wacky wheel suddenly changed direction and chased the scientists instead.

4 THE TERRIBLE TREADMILL (1817)
EVIL RATING - A well-rounded invention!
There's nothing better than
watching my enemies suffer
with my giant hamster
wheel, which turns as they
climb the steps. It was
used on Victorian prisoners,
and inventor William Cubitt
added a brake to make the
wheel harder to turn. The
effort was equal to climbing a mountain every day
and prisoners weren't allowed to talk. Oh well, at
least it kept them fit, heh heh!

STEP ON IT!

3 THE TERRIFYING THUMBSCREWS
(17TH CENTURY)
EVIL RATING - You've got to hand it to them...
For torturers on the go,
this invention was easy
to carry. The screw turned
to crush the victim's
fingernails, but I think that
sounds quite nice compared
to a German version that
crushed the victim's skull.
Let's hope the torturers
didn't have a screw loose.

ARRRGH! OK, OK!
I GIVE THEM THE
THUMBS UP!

CRUNCH!

2 THE REVOLTING RACK (16TH CENTURY)
EVIL RATING - A good way to stretch your legs.
I love seeing my enemies at full stretch ... the rack

was used throughout Europe and I suppose the victim would go to any lengths to escape it...

LEVERS TIGHTENED ROPES AND STRETCHED THE VICTIM UNTIL THEIR BONES PLOPPED OUT OF THEIR SOCKETS.

STRETCH!

YOU'RE GOING DOWN FOR A LONG STRETCH, MATEY!

THE *GUILLOTINE* (16TH CENTURY ONWARDS)
EVIL RATING - You might feel a bit cut up.

HINGED BOARD FOR LYING ON IS A LEVER, SO IS THE BOARD FOR HOLDING THE HEAD STEADY

TUT TUT — SOMEONE'S FORGOTTEN TO CLEAN THE BLOODSTAINS OFF THE BLADE.

DON'T LOSE YOUR HEAD!

DO I HAVE A CHOICE?

NICE WOODWORK

FOUR FEARFUL GUILLOTINE FACTS TO SHARPEN YOUR WITS ON

1 The guillotine was NOT invented by French doctor Joseph-Ignace Guillotin in 1789. He simply told the National Assembly that it would be a kinder way to execute people. Everyone laughed, but during the French Revolution the government needed a machine to chop heads off in a hurry. In ten years 15,000 people were killed in this way.

2 The first victim of the French guillotine was highway robber Nicolas Pelletier. The executioner Charles Sanson took his work very seriously and practised beforehand on animals

62

and dead bodies. You'll be delighted to know that it all came together at the execution, except for Pelletier, who came apart. A delighted Dr G was heard to remark:

THE VICTIM DID NOT SUFFER AT ALL. HE WAS CONSCIOUS OF NO MORE THAN A SLIGHT CHILL ON THE NECK.

THE VICTIM DIDN'T CHALLENGE DR G'S COMMENT.

Mind you, that was before his head fell off. Is that one chill-out session you could do without?

3 Before Dr G, there had been guillotine-type machines in Italy, Britain and Ireland. In Halifax, England, for example, the people in the crowd released the guillotine blade so everyone could join in the fun. Sometimes when a thief stole a sheep, the sheep did the job of releasing the blade.

4 In 1564 the Earl of Morton took the idea to Scotland. But when he fell from power, he had his head cut off by his own killing machine.

And on that note we'd better change the subject and look at something hot and spluttering that could blow up at any moment.

STAGGERING STEAM TRAINS

Steam trains might seem old-fashioned today but in their time they were the height of technology – so let's let off some steam and hope we don't go off the rails…

TRAIN-SPOTTING TEACHER'S
TEA-BREAK TEASER
Knock ever so softly on the
staffroom door. Ask your teacher:

a) Stone Age people.
b) Ancient Greeks.
c) Someone in the Middle Ages.
d) The Victorians.

ANSWER

b) AND **c)** And the teacher is only allowed a gold star if she gets the answer EXACTLY RIGHT! **b)** The ancient Greeks moved ships on rails across the Isthmus of Corinth (a narrow neck of land in Greece). **c)** Mine owners all over Europe built railways to shift loads in the mines – the wagons were pulled by ponies or even people.

A successful railway needed one more invention – an engine to pull the wagons. Lots of inventors worked on the idea, but the first to succeed was a bit of a strong character. In fact he was so strong that he could pick your teacher up and turn them upside down. His name was Richard Trevithick (1771–1833), and we've turned his exciting life into a play…

RECKLESS RICHARD

ACT 1

(A PUB IN CORNWALL IN 1801. RT IS TALKING TO THE LANDLORD.)

NARRATOR: Richard Trevithick was the strongest man in Cornwall. He threw mighty sledgehammers and turned grown men upside down for fun. He was also a brilliant inventor...

LANDLORD: So is it true you've invented a steam-powered car?

RT: It's true – hic!

(RATHER DRUNK) I've just left it parked down the street with the fire still burning.

LANDLORD: Will it be all right?

RT: Of course it will – hic!

(WE HEAR THE SOUND OF A MUFFLED EXPLOSION)

BOOOOFFF!

RT: As long as I don't let the boiler run dry!

ACT 2

(THE PENYDARREN IRONWORKS IN WALES 1804)

SCENE 1:

ENTER SAMUEL HOMFRAY, ANTHONY HILL AND RT.

AH: And I bet you can't carry coal and people by railway!

67

SH: And I bet I can – with the help of Mr Trevithick's newly invented steam locomotive.

RT: (SMUGLY) My invention can do the job easily!

SCENE 2: LATER THAT DAY

SH: I still say I won the bet!

AH: And I still say I won because the loco broke the rails and had to travel back by road.

RT: Well, at least it was the world's first train-passenger journey!

SH: I'm not so chuff-chuffed about that!

ACT 3

(A HOTEL IN COLUMBIA, SOUTH AMERICA IN 1827)
ENTER ROBERT STEPHENSON AND RT

RS: Fancy bumping into you, Mr Trevithick! So what have you been up to all these years?

RT : (FEELING SORRY FOR HIMSELF) My whole life has been a failure! I failed at school, my steam car blew up, and no one wanted my steam locomotive. I came here to South America to work in mining – but my work failed. I nearly starved and had to eat monkeys, I nearly drowned, I nearly got eaten by an alligator and I'm nearly skint...

RS: Cheer up Mr Trevithick! Since you've been away railways have become popular. My dad, George Stephenson, improved your loco with a blast pipe that made the furnace hotter so it burnt coal better and now he's rich and famous. Isn't that good news?

RT: Grr – your dad pinched my idea and you're telling me to cheer up!

RS: I'll pay for your ticket home…

RT: Oh all right!

EXIT RS AND RT ARM IN ARM.

NARRATOR: A few years later, Richard Trevithick died without a penny to his name.

R·I·P
Richard
Trevithick
Born **1771**
Ran out
of steam
1833

(CURTAIN FALLS – BOOS AND HISSES AND ROTTEN TOMATOES THROWN BY THE AUDIENCE.)

69

BET YOU NEVER KNEW!

Train engineers used a boring machine to make boilers from solid cylinders. The inventor was John "iron-mad" Wilkinson, who hit on the machine in 1775. John was so mad on iron that he was buried in an iron coffin under an iron monument. And by the way, his machine wasn't at all boring – it was quite interesting really.

PROFESSOR Z GETS ALL STEAMED UP

We asked Professor Z to explain how the steam engine worked.

IF YOU HEAT WATER IN A BOILER THE FORCE OF THE STEAM POWERS PISTONS WHICH TURN GEARS THAT TURN THE TRAIN'S WHEELS...

CHUG CHUG!

TERRIBLE TRAIN TRAVEL

If you wanted to travel by train in the early days, the best advice would have been "DON'T!" Early trains were DANGEROUS with a capital "D", and it was only a matter of time before they claimed their first victim… This tragic event happened in 1830. A young girl named Frances Kemble was on the train and this is how she might have told the story…

MY FIRST TRAIN JOURNEY
BY FRANCES KEMBLE

I'll never forget my first train journey. It happened last Wednesday when Mama and I were fortunate enough to get tickets for the opening of the new Liverpool to Manchester railway.

My heart was in my mouth as we joined the excited crowd at the new Liverpool station. I gazed open-mouthed at the big black shiny, chuffing, engines - they seemed more the work of gods than humans. One of them gave a blast of steam with a spine-tingling whistle, and I almost screamed in terror.

Suddenly a loud cannon blast shook the station. It was the signal for our journey to begin and we all clambered into open wagons and carriages - and some people sat on top of the coal wagons. Mama and I became separated. I sat in a wagon next to a man who said that the cannon blast had hit a man and made his eyeball fall out. I shuddered.

As we moved off I gripped my seat and hung on tight, and the faster we moved the tighter I held on. But soon I had forgotten all about that poor man and his eyeball. I was too busy waving at the crowds who lined the way and waving at men on horses and coaches that tried to keep up with us but kept getting left behind. I felt like a princess. I loved watching the streets and fields go flying past and listening to the loud chuffing of our engine and sniffing the stinky sooty smell of the smoke.

At last we stopped. It was time to take on more water for the engine. One of the railway men shouted that we were to stay in our wagons but no one took any notice. Lots of people opened the doors and climbed down onto the railway. I wanted to stretch my legs and find

Mama and ask her what she thought of the trip. But when at last I found her she looked as white as chalk and she had her handkerchief over her mouth as if she was about to be sick.

"What's wrong, Mama?" I cried.

"It's that locomotive - it frightens me!" she moaned.

"But, Mama," I said, taking her arm. "It's so exciting!"

Mama led me to the carriage where she was sitting. She had arranged with a man who was sitting next to her to swap seats with me, so we could sit together. No sooner had we taken our places than other people began to clamber into our carriage and I heard the thunderous roar of a second engine approaching. With a shriek the big black engine flashed past, and all at once I heard a man's shout and a woman's scream. I found out later that some people hadn't got back on the train fast enough and soon people were saying in low voices that someone had been hit.

Mama's friend Lady Wilton had seen it all. When we met her at Manchester station at the end of the journey, poor Lady W was looking as green as her dress.

"It was Mr Huskisson!" she sobbed. "He was a bit lame. No one helped him into the carriage and there he was hanging from the door when the engine hit him. He fell and the engine ran over his leg. I can still hear the bone cracking and poor Mr Huskisson groaning that it was all over for him. Oh it was a horrible sight - I feel quite unwell..."

Mama winced and began to tremble and Lord Wilton looked scarcely better than his wife.

"Hush my dear, do not alarm yourself," he soothed. "It is over now and at least I'm safe although I did have to hide behind a wagon."

Oddly enough, her husband's narrow escape did not cheer Lady W in the least bit - and she sobbed harder than ever and looked about to burst into hysterics.

"Where is Mr Huskisson now, Your Lordship?" I asked politely.

"He is being cared for in a nearby village. Our driver was Mr George Stephenson, railway engineer. After the accident he was very brave. He uncoupled our engine and set off at high speed with Mr Huskisson, but I fear he won't live."

G.S.

"That's the last time I ever travel by train. Nasty, dirty, smelly, noisy, dangerous things!" said Mama bitterly. "I too, dear," said Lady W, pulling herself together with a shudder and a sniff.

What a pity, I thought, not daring to voice my opinions. Apart from the accident and that poor man's eyeball it had been a really exciting day. I can't wait to go on a train again!

TERRIBLE TRAINS

And you'll be sorry to read that top politician William Huskisson died of his injuries. He was the first of many and here's why...

There were no signals to stop trains smashing into each other on the same length of track. In Britain the guard had to sit in a little hut on top of a train carriage and be ready to stop the train in an emergency. (The train brakes were blocks that jammed up against the wheels.) Of course he ended up with a face full of soot. In the USA the brakeman had to run along the top of the train to operate the brakes — and some men got their heads chopped off when the trains went into tunnels.

BRITISH GUARD

AMERICAN BRAKEMAN

Engine-boiler explosions were common in the early days. The first American loco was the *Best Friend of Charleston*. Sadly the man who stoked the fire decided to eat his lunch sitting on top of the boiler steam valve, which had to be kept clear. One horribly huge blast later, all that was left were a few bits of metal and a few bits of the man. Hmm – with "best friends" like that who needs enemies?

But where there's a problem, there's often an army of inventors trying to invent an answer. Here's one sensible idea that really worked and one idea that was as silly as a dog's book of table manners...

THE SENSIBLE INVENTION

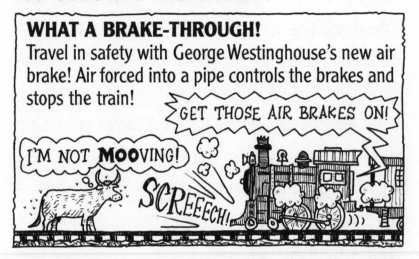

In 1869 US inventor George Westinghouse (1846–1914) tried to get rail bosses to back his invention. Then during a test, a man fell in front of the train. George's brake stopped the train and saved the man's life. The shaken bosses bought the brake.

THE SILLY INVENTION

WORRIED ABOUT TRAIN ACCIDENTS?

Why not leap aboard the leapfrog train? Our trains have a sloping front with a railway track built on top of them. If they collide, one train rides over the other. It's more fun than a theme park!

US inventor RK Stern dreamt up this idiotic invention in 1905. To prove it worked, he ran it as a fairground ride. And – yes, it did work, but it was so scary that no one wanted to try it twice. And if the two trains weren't going at the same speed they still crashed.

Of course steam engines were used for loads of other inventions besides trains. For example, they powered the weaving machines that thousands of Victorian children ended up working at for long hours. And in 1893 inventor George Moore even built a steam-powered robot. This metal monster walked three times faster than a real man and puffed steam through a metal cigar. So could you design a steam-powered mechanical teacher? Hmm – better not. Your machine might get steamed up and blow a gasket (just like a real teacher).

And then there were steam-powered boats. One of the first was built by Marquis Jouffroy d'Abbans in

1776. But sadly his boat, built with paddles shaped like duck's feet, proved to be a dead duck. It didn't move – perhaps because it lacked engine power – and a later version fell to bits. The miserable Marquis lost his money and ended up as broke as his machine.

But the idea was good, and in 1807 inventor Robert Fulton ran the first passenger steamboat service in the USA. Steam-powered ships followed.

We're taking a break now for some more awful adverts. But don't go away, because after the adverts we'll be looking at more weird watercraft and finding out why boffins tried to train seagulls to poo on submarines…

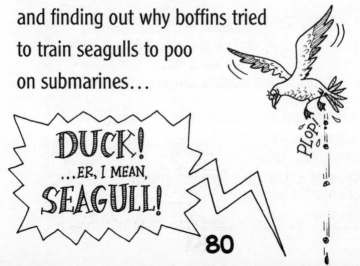

DUCK!
…ER, I MEAN,
SEAGULL!

PLOP!

AWFUL ADVERTISEMENTS 2

Idiotic inventors have always taken a hands-on approach to fun, fashion and fitness, so let's check out some of their inventions that never quite got off the ground...

FANCY A CHALLENGE?

Try this plastic exercise suit! (USA 1998)
• Special cords make any movement require extra effort.
• It's just like being tied up!
• Lovely choice of colours!

The small print

1 British students who tested a similar suit ended up over-heating and fainting.

2 You look like a giant baby.

3 If you pay extra we might help you escape from it!

GNNNN!

WATCH THE BIRDIE!

Now you can shoot duck in comfort! All you have to do is dress up as a giant duck. The real ducks will be helpless with laughter and you'll be able to catch them easily!

WARNING! Make sure there are no short-sighted hunters in the area – they might mistake you for a real duck!

I DOUBT IT!

IT'S WHEELIE FUN! We've got loads of ideas for fun on wheels (hospital bills not included)…

THE WHEELIE WONDER (USA 2004)

You're strapped to a set of wheels and go whizzing down a really steep hill!

**ARTIST COMING THROUGH!*

BE A BATTY BATMAN! (USA 1996)

Are you just a bit too cool? You won't be with this batty bat cape and roller-skate outfit. All you do is flap your wings, skate along and try to ignore the crowd of people laughing at you!

Don't get wet, try…

THE ZIPPY-BAG SPECTATOR PROTECTOR

WHAT'RE YOU STARING AT?

Why should a drop of rain spoil the big match? Simply zip yourself up in a giant bag and watch in comfort. Plus you're sure to have lots of space because no one will want to sit next to you!

*SEE PAGE 4

DON'T BE A DRIP!!!
Stay dry in the street with the...

PERSONAL SHOWER CURTAIN
(USA 1995)

INFLATABLE SHOWER CAP

DON'T FORGET TO WEAR CLOTHES!

Dogs needn't get a soaking either!
Just buy them a trendy

DOGGIE UMBRELLA
(USA 1992)

BREATHING HOLES = <u>VERY</u> IMPORTANT

EAR WE GO AGAIN!
Ears are so boring aren't they? But now you can make your ears the centre of attention with these exciting new inventions!

JUST WING IT! USA 1991)
No one will laugh at your ears again with these wonderful ear-wings (they'll be too busy laughing at your ear-covers instead!).

WEIRD!

CHEERS BIG EARS!
(Europe 1973)

Scientists say that big ears hear better – so why not wear a pair of giant ears? They're great for grumpy grannies and anyone who ever wanted to be a rabbit.

YOU CAN EVEN WIGGLE YOUR EARS TO POINT IN DIFFERENT DIRECTIONS.

HATS TO DIE FOR!
(Well, you might die of embarrassment first!)

THE BLIND SPOT HAT (USA 1994)

Instructions for use
1 Close your left eye and focus on the dangling toy with your right eye.
2 Now switch eyes and the toy will disappear. That's because you're looking at it with your blind spot (the point where the nerves to your brain leave your eyeball).
It's fun for all the family,

REQUIRES GREAT CONCENTRATION

and your teacher is sure to enjoy the sight of you grinning and winking at her in science lessons!

THE BIG HAIR POINTY-HAT
(USA 1962)

It's the perfect shower cap for ladies who want to keep their "big hair" dry in the shower! It's also ideal for aliens, unicorns, giant squid and anyone else with a funny pointy head.

GO AWAY!

BANISH BOREDOM WITH THE
GOOFY GERBIL FUN SHIRT!
(USA 1999)

Now you can turn your shirt into the perfect pet playground! It's guaranteed to liven up a boring science lesson!

• Gary the gerbil will LURVE scampering through the tubes in your shirt and there are even air holes so he can breathe.

• Play "spot that gerbil" with your friends!

• For added thrills why not let your pet python into the tubes and watch him slither after Gary!

I'M BEGINNING TO WISH I HADN'T WRITTEN THIS BIT!*

*SEE PAGE 4

85

SINKING SUBS (AND OTHER SEA AND AIR INVENTIONS)

Wouldn't it be c-o-o-l to invent your own submarine? You could take your family on underwater cruises and make friends with sharks. And if you were an evil inventor you might take your enemies on underwater cruises and feed them to sharks. Mind you, submarines do have their bad side for inventors. If your sub doesn't work properly you might find yourself stuck on the seabed with no way of escape and your air running out…

Modern subs can suffer alarming accidents, but early subs were dodgy death traps that were more dangerous to the people who sailed in them than anyone else. And who better to sell us one than a man who claims every clapped-out banger is "a classic car" – my very untruthful mate Honest Bob…

CONTINUED...

87

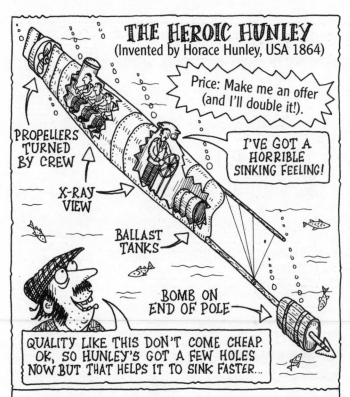

THE HEROIC HUNLEY
(Invented by Horace Hunley, USA 1864)

Price: Make me an offer (and I'll double it!).

I'VE GOT A HORRIBLE SINKING FEELING!

PROPELLERS TURNED BY CREW

X-RAY VIEW

BALLAST TANKS

BOMB ON END OF POLE

QUALITY LIKE THIS DON'T COME CHEAP. OK, SO HUNLEY'S GOT A FEW HOLES NOW BUT THAT HELPS IT TO SINK FASTER...

THE SMALL PRINT - 1 The Hunley was tested three times. Each time it sank and one test killed its inventor. 2 A crew of valiant volunteers sailed the sub to attack a ship belonging to the Union side in the American Civil War. The ship sank, but sadly so did the sub, and the entire crew were killed.

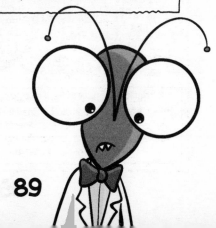

Several Victorian inventors worked on submarines. But today's subs are descended from the vessel built by an Irish-born ex-teacher named John Holland (1841–1914). Holland later had doubts about the destructive power of his invention but it was too late. In the First and Second World Wars, submarines sank hundreds of ships and killed many thousands of people.

BET YOU NEVER KNEW!

In the First World War British boffins were so desperate to defeat German subs that they tried some odd ideas...

PLAN A – Patrol ports in small boats. Each boat carries swimmers who try to put a bag over the periscope so the Germans in the sub can't see.

PLAN B – If that doesn't work break the periscope glass with a hammer.

PLAN C – Train seagulls to poo on the periscopes.

All these potty plans were as sensible as organizing a teddy bears' picnic with real bears.

SINISTER SUB SECRETS

We decided to join Professor Z and Nora on board the Prof's evil submarine to find out how it works…

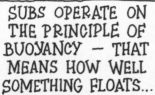

SUBS OPERATE ON THE PRINCIPLE OF BUOYANCY — THAT MEANS HOW WELL SOMETHING FLOATS…

PUT AN OBJECT IN WATER AND IT DISPLACES (THAT MEANS PUSHES ASIDE) ITS VOLUME IN WATER…

WITH AIR IN ITS BALLAST TANKS, MY SUB IS LIGHTER THAN ITS VOLUME OF WATER. THIS MEANS IT'S BUOYANT — THE WATER SUPPORTS IT AND IT FLOATS.

SINKING SHIPS AND LIFESAVING LIGHTHOUSES

Even before inventors thought of subs, ships had a horrible habit of sinking without help. They sank in storms, or got wrecked on rocks. And that's why someone invented lighthouses. There were lighthouses in the Mediterranean Sea from ancient times and I guess they were a bright idea and a shining example and ... (that's enough light-hearted jokes – the editor). Here's how a newspaper might have told the story of a famous English lighthouse...

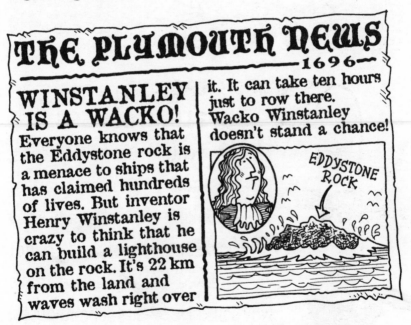

THE PLYMOUTH NEWS
—1696—

WINSTANLEY IS A WACKO!

Everyone knows that the Eddystone rock is a menace to ships that has claimed hundreds of lives. But inventor Henry Winstanley is crazy to think that he can build a lighthouse on the rock. It's 22 km from the land and waves wash right over it. It can take ten hours just to row there. Wacko Winstanley doesn't stand a chance!

EDDYSTONE ROCK

THE PLYMOUTH NEWS
—1698—

HENRY IS A HERO!

All Plymouth is singing the praises of hero Henry Winstanley. He's risked his life to build a lighthouse and for the first time ships can see the Eddystone rock in the dark.

Tonight the pubs are packed with happy sailors crying with joy as they drink the health of this incredible inventor! Stop Press! Some miserable moaners claim the lighthouse won't survive a bad storm, but Winstanley says he wants to be there during the worst storm ever. We bet the moaners will run out of puff then!

THE PLYMOUTH NEWS
—1703—

WINSTANLEY WASHED AWAY!

Winstanley set off to repair the lighthouse yesterday. Last night was the most terrible storm ever. Hundreds of ships have been lost and 8,000 sailors are feared drowned. Today all eyes turned to Winstanley's lighthouse. But it had gone. All that remains of his beautiful tower are a few jagged bits of metal. It's now certain that Winstanley and his entire crew are dead. But these men died to make our seas safe and we won't forget them!!

In time, engineer John Smeaton built a new lighthouse on the rock, and you'll be dancing with joy to read that ever since then there has been a lighthouse on the Eddystone rock. Mind you, even with the best lighthouses in the world some ships should never have been invented…

THE HORRIBLE SCIENCE SILLY SHIP COMPETITION
Anti-seasickness ship (1875)

CABIN STAYS LEVEL WHILE THE REST OF THE SHIP ROLLS WITH THE WAVES

BIG WAVE!

OK... HELLO!

4th prize

X-RAY VIEW

Judge's report

Henry Bessemer was famous for inventing a new steel-making method. But his ship was a disaster. It didn't steer well and demolished the pier at Calais ... twice.

Giant boat ball (1973)

Judge's report

The American inventor of this boat must have been on a bit of a roll – but we think it would have been impossible to steer. Luckily it was never built.

Incredible round ship (1873)

2 TEN-TONNE GUNS

2nd prize

WE'LL RUN CIRCLES ROUND THEM!

12 PROPELLERS

Judge's report

This ship was actually built by Admiral Popov of the Russian Navy. It could sail forwards, backwards and even spin around (in fact we felt quite seasick). The other problem was that you couldn't steer it very well.

Giant iceberg ship (1944)

AIRCRAFT CARRIER, 800 METRES LONG

GREAT IN A COLD WAR!

1st prize

MADE FROM ICE MIXED WITH TINY BITS OF WOOD

Judge's report

A ship built of ice – we love it! British boffin Geoffrey Pyke came up with the idea, and a scaled-down trial version was built in Canada.

The incredible inventor of the iceberg ship had an incredible life. During the First World War gallant Geoffrey decided to report the war ... from the

German side. The Germans nearly shot him as a spy before he escaped. Geoff said that his prison wasn't as tough as his brutal boarding school. And after the war he decided to open a better kind of school.

New School Rules
By Geoffrey Pyke
1. There are no punishments for pupils — not even a telling off.
2. Pupils don't have to go to lessons.
3. Pupils can learn whatever they like.

COOL!

Children LOVED the new school, but for some strange reason their killjoy parents didn't and the school shut down. But the school was just one of genius Geoff's brilliant brainwaves...

The Incredible Inventor Files

NAME: Geoffrey Pyke
(1893–1948)

NATIONALITY: British

CLAIM TO FAME: With his scruffy beard, shabby suit and sockless shoes, Geoffrey Pyke looked the spitting image of a mad scientist – and that's not surprising because he was a mad scientist!

INCREDIBLE INVENTIONS: Geoffrey had always loved inventions and he'd already invented a pedal-powered train. During the Second World War he invented crazy contraptions such as the icy aircraft carrier to help the war effort.

DREADFUL DETAILS: One of his motorized sledge inventions was cunningly disguised as a toilet. Another of his ideas was to send supplies and PEOPLE through pipes.

DON'T MENTION: After the war, the government ignored Geoffrey's odd ideas. In fact he was laughed at.

AWFUL END: At last, feeling sad and lonely, the scientist shaved off his beard and swallowed a bottle of sleeping pills. So ended his incredibly inventive life.

HOW TO BUILD A GIANT ICY AIRCRAFT CARRIER

The giant icy aircraft carrier wasn't as silly as it sounds. If you freeze water and tiny bits of wood, the ice becomes incredibly strong and melts less easily. Geoffrey's giant ship would have been so huge it would have been impossible to sink. It was even fitted with super-cooled water guns that could squirt an attacking ship and freeze it into a block of ice.

FREEZE!

YARGH!

K-BOOSH!

YOU'RE SUPPOSED TO SAY THAT **BEFORE** YOU SHOOT!

Military planner Louis Mountbatten backed the idea, and he dropped the ice in Prime Minister Winston Churchill's bath to prove it wouldn't melt.

To show how strong the material was, loopy Louis fired his gun at it in a top military meeting. The bullet bounced off and nearly killed an Admiral. But sadly, despite the building of the scaled-down version, there wasn't enough time or money to build the full-sized aircraft carrier before the war ended. So I guess the plans were "put on ice".

Talking about aircraft carriers, I really ought to mention some awesome aircraft inventions...

AN URGENT MESSAGE FROM THE AUTHOR

I could tell you loads and loads about planes and how they were invented and the science of flight, but I'm not going to because...

1. I might end up writing a Horrible Science book full of wacky aircraft.

2. I've already written that book.

So instead here's an exclusive peek inside the Horrible Science awful aircraft museum.

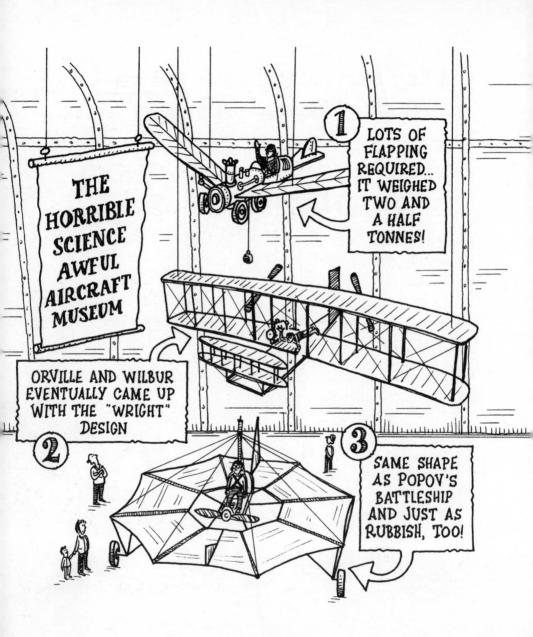

THE HORRIBLE SCIENCE AWFUL AIRCRAFT MUSEUM

1 LOTS OF FLAPPING REQUIRED... IT WEIGHED TWO AND A HALF TONNES!

2 ORVILLE AND WILBUR EVENTUALLY CAME UP WITH THE "WRIGHT" DESIGN

3 SAME SHAPE AS POPOV'S BATTLESHIP AND JUST AS RUBBISH, TOO!

105

1 Joseph Kaufmann's steam-powered plane (1869). No steam-powered plane ever flew because their engines were too heavy. This one was based on a bumblebee. It was meant to flap its wings and fly but the wings only flapped until they fell off. I guess the inventor got in a flap instead...

2 Orville and Wilbur Wright's "Flyer" (1903). This petrol-powered plane was the first to fly successfully. Sadly it was also the first plane to crash. The Flyer had no brakes and no safety belt and in 1908 it hit the ground, killing a passenger.

3 Chance Vought's umbrella plane (1911). This potty plane didn't go anywhere at all but at least you could sit under it and shelter from the rain.

4 The flying jeep (1942). British scientists in the Second World War built a jeep with a kind of helicopter blade on top. Early tests nearly killed its pilot and the project was dropped even faster than the plane.

5 The NASA space shuttle (1981) is the most complex flying machine ever – it's designed to take off like a rocket, fly in space and land like an aircraft. Most missions were successful, but in 1986 and 2003 shuttles blew up killing their crews.

BET YOU NEVER KNEW!

In 1997 a US inventor came up with a craft that might have replaced all the subs and ships and planes in this chapter and here it is...

This flying saucer sub was supposed to whizz 11.6 km in the air and sail beneath the waves. There was even a parachute for those little emergencies. Sadly this magnificent machine wasn't built owing to the awkward fact that it wouldn't have worked.

But cheer up – if you're late for school you can always travel by road instead. And in the next chapter there's an invention that might just get you there on time. But you'd better hurry up – the driver's getting impatient...

CRAZY CARS

When it comes to getting around, two legs are never good enough for inventors. They prefer to dream up machines that go ever faster, even if some of them are on the mad side of crazy. Our story really starts with steam-powered cars…

Remember Richard Trevithick's exploding steam car? Well that wasn't the only steam car setback. Travelling by steam-powered car was as sensible as picnicking on top of a volcano – they really did seem to be jinxed…

FOUR STEAM CAR SETBACKS

1 In 1769 French inventor Nicolas Cugnot built a steam car that ended up crashing into a wall. It was the first car crash in history.

2 In the USA Oliver Evans was laughed at for designing steam cars. Then he fell out with one of his workers who burned down his factory.

3 In England inventor Goldsworthy Gurney lost a fortune trying to run a steam-car passenger service. When he tried to show off the car to a top official they were attacked by an anti-government crowd and the inventor was beaten up.

4 A similar steam car in Scotland was sabotaged – possibly by people who ran horse-drawn coaches.

Its wheels gave way, its boiler blew up and four passengers were killed.

Eventually, like trains, steam cars became faster and safer, and in 1906 a steam-powered car set the world-speed record. The Stanley Steamer steamed ahead at 205.5 km per hour – but by then petrol-driven cars had been invented and were becoming more and more successful. As you can see, the story of the car was full of surprises and wrong turnings so here's a road map to help you find your way…

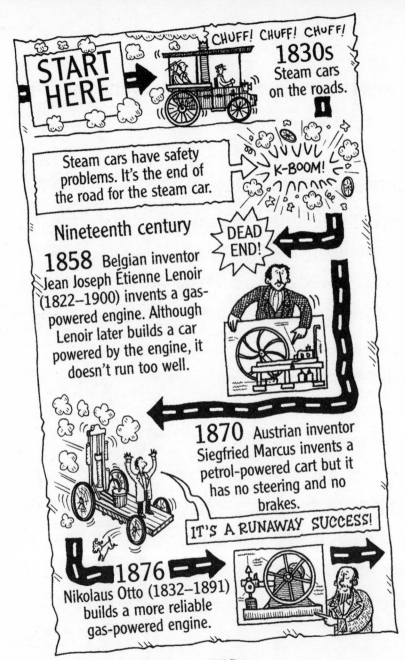

START HERE

CHUFF! CHUFF! CHUFF!

1830s Steam cars on the roads.

Steam cars have safety problems. It's the end of the road for the steam car.

K-BOOM!

DEAD END!

Nineteenth century

1858 Belgian inventor Jean Joseph Étienne Lenoir (1822–1900) invents a gas-powered engine. Although Lenoir later builds a car powered by the engine, it doesn't run too well.

1870 Austrian inventor Siegfried Marcus invents a petrol-powered cart but it has no steering and no brakes.

IT'S A RUNAWAY SUCCESS!

1876 Nikolaus Otto (1832–1891) builds a more reliable gas-powered engine.

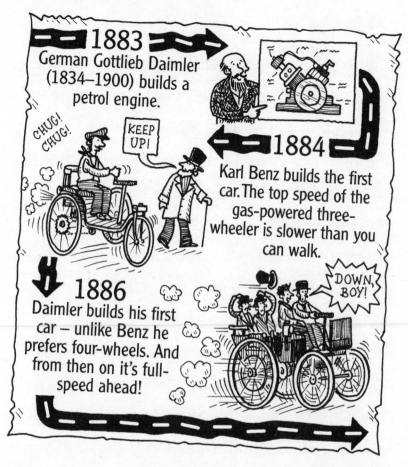

1883

German Gottlieb Daimler (1834–1900) builds a petrol engine.

CHUG! CHUG!

KEEP UP!

1884

Karl Benz builds the first car. The top speed of the gas-powered three-wheeler is slower than you can walk.

1886

Daimler builds his first car – unlike Benz he prefers four-wheels. And from then on it's full-speed ahead!

DOWN, BOY!

But that still wasn't very fast. Until 1896 British cars followed a man on foot carrying a red flag to warn other road users. And that was just the start of their troubles. Early cars were hard to start – you had to crank a handle that sometimes slipped and knocked your teeth out. And even when you managed to get moving you froze in the open car and didn't get very far before you broke down. No wonder Gottlieb Daimler died after a winter drive in one of his cars. And no wonder the first long-distance car journey was a bit of an adventure. But an intrepid inventor didn't make this epic drive – it was made by a mum and her two children.

Bertha Benz was the driving force (geddit?) behind hubbie, Karl. She gave him money for his work at a time when people hung around his workshop waiting for his cars to crash. One day Mrs B decided to show everyone that the car had a great future. She planned to drive to her mum's house over 80 km away without telling Karl. Here's how her younger son might have remembered the trip.

MY HOMEWORK
by Richard Benz

August 1888

Yesterday Mum borrowed Dad's car and drove us to our granny's. Me and my brother Eugene had to get up early and tiptoe out of the house so we didn't wake Dad. Then we helped Mum push the car out of Dad's workshop.

It wasn't until we were sitting in the car that we realized we had a few problems. None of us knew how to start the car - or drive it. And Mum didn't know the way.

We got the car going in the end - Mum always manages things - and off we went. The roads were bumpy and dusty and we had to stop at a chemist's* to buy dry-cleaning fluid to use as fuel. And that's not all. The water to cool the engine kept running dry so we had to stop for water all the time and Mum made me scoop water from a dirty ditch - UGH!

*There were no garages at the time!

115

The werst [or] bit was the hills.
Me and my brother had to
get out and push the car.
And coming down the hills
was skary [c] because the
brakes burnt out and Mum
had to get a shoemaker to

WHAT A LOVELY VIEW!

mend them. But nothing stops Mum! She
mended a broyken spring with elastic from
her underwear and when the fooel [u] pipe
blocked she unblocked it with her hatpin.

OOER!

Then we hit another problem. It
began to get dark, and Dad's
car has no lights. Luckily local
people from Pforzheim came out
with lantins [er] to show us the
way. By then we were tired out
and dirty and dusty. But Mum was happy.
She says she knew the car could do it and
she can't wait to drive home again. Next
time I think I'll get the train.

A good story but I
don't believe a word of it!   C+

Five days later Bertha drove the kids home to hubbie who by then had noticed that his precious invention had gone missing. But talking about engine problems – are you just itching to know how cars work? Well, if you are itching you really ought to scratch yourself and if you're not, it's probably because you're not an oily engineer.

AN EVIL WAY TO FIND OUT HOW CARS WORK

The Professor's cut a car in half to show us how it works. Hmm – maybe he should have asked the owner first!

CHAINSAW, INVENTED BY
ANDREAS STIHL IN 1926

Numbers on diagram:

1 Four-cylinder internal-combustion engine.

2 Engine turns gears and gears turn prop shaft.

3 Prop shaft powers rear wheels.

4 Streamlined shape allows air to flow easily around the car when driving at speed. This allows it to go faster and use less fuel.

5 Column of steering wheel linked to a rod and gears to control steering.

6 Air bag fills with gas in less than one-tenth of a second and protects the driver in a crash. Hmm – it looks like this driver could do with a bit of protection from Professor Z!

7 Catalytic converter. Removes some of the nastier waste gases from the engine such as carbon monoxide.

8 Fuel tank – it's a good idea to keep this away from the hot engine.

9 Differential box – as the car turns, the wheels on one side need to travel further and that means they need to turn faster. This brilliant box allows it to happen.

EVERYTHING YOU EVER WANTED TO KNOW ABOUT THE INTERNAL-COMBUSTION ENGINE...

It gets its name because combustion (a posh word for burning fuel) takes place inside the engine. In a steam engine, combustion takes place in a furnace outside the engine and that makes it an external-combustion engine.

Inside the engine cylinder, exploding fuel powers a piston. The piston movements are called "the four-stroke cycle" but they're nothing to do with stroking cats or cycling bikes.

Most car engines are actually powered by several cylinders. The more cylinders they have the more powerful they are.

The sparks that explode the fuel are made by electric spark-plugs. Now that's what I call "a flash of inspiration".

In fact not all cars have the same sort of engine. Some cars and most lorries and buses have diesel engines, invented by a man who met a mysterious and possibly evil end...

MISSING PERSON REPORT

By Inspector Clueless of the Missing Persons Department

NAME: Rudolf Diesel

PROFESSION: Inventor

DATE: October 1913

BACKGROUND: Diesel is well-known for inventing the diesel engine in 1892. The advantage of this engine is that by squeezing air in the cylinder, air gets hot enough to set fire to the fuel it burns. The engine needs no spark plugs and it's cheaper to run than a petrol engine.

PERSONAL PROBLEMS: Diesel wasn't very lucky. He built a coal-dust burning engine that blew up and nearly killed him. He'd lost most of his money in dodgy business deals...

DISAPPEARANCE: Diesel was on his way to England to sell his invention to the British navy. He disappeared from the ship. Some German fishermen say they found his body but they left it in the sea. So what really happened? Did Diesel mean to take his own life? My police colleagues think he did but perhaps there is a more sinister explanation. Britain and Germany are heading for war. Perhaps someone wanted Diesel dead before he could sell his secrets to the British? The whole business smells fishy — but not as fishy as Diesel when they found him floating in the sea...

'DIESEL' SPOIL OUR FISHING TRIP!

YAR, LEEF 'IM IN ZEE VATER!

121

By 1913, the car was already on its way to conquering the world. As ever with a new invention, the design of the car got better and better. In 1894 cars could chug along at the speed of a horse, but within ten years they were whizzing along at 160 km per hour.

BEFORE　　　　AFTER

And not just cars. In time, Rudolf Diesel's engine proved ideal for lorries and buses. And internal-combustion engines proved light enough to power motorbikes (from 1885) and even boats with an outboard motor.

BET YOU NEVER KNEW!

1   Norwegian-born inventor Ole Evinrude invented the outboard motor in the USA. One day in 1906 Ole rowed his girlfriend, Bess, to an island in a lake. Bess fancied an ice cream so Ole gallantly rowed four kilometres to the shore and back ... only to find that the ice cream had

melted. Exhausted Ole vowed to build an engine linked to a propeller to power a boat.

2 And that's not the only romantic story about an outboard motor. In 2002 Bruce the goose from British Columbia fell in LOVE with an outboard motor. Instead of flying off with his feathered friends, the brainless bird preferred to stand around with the motorized love of his life...

Today some *people* seem to be in love with their motors – and that goes for inventors too. They've dreamt up some completely crazy car contraptions. But which of these dodgy discoveries are a little too crazy to be true?

CRAZY CAR QUIZ

TRUE or FALSE?

1 A car engine powered a machine that blasted an 18-metre wall of flame for movies.

2 A car for dogs. The specially built "mutt-mobile" features pedals for paws, a nose-operated steering wheel and a free CD of dogs barking to music.

3 A motorized picnic table. Now you can explore the scenery as you scoff your sandwiches.

4 A car with an automatic dishwasher strapped to one wheel.

5 A car that pulls faces and cries.

6 A car with an on-board toilet.

1 TRUE – it was dreamt up by Cliff Richardson in the 1970s. The engine powers a fuel pump and the fuel is set on fire. It sounds a real blast but NO – you won't be allowed to try it in a science lesson!

2 FALSE – Rover cars are nothing to do with dogs and if you try teaching your pet to drive you're sure to be "hounded" by the cops.

3 TRUE – in 2003 a US inventor came up with a motorized table and benches on wheels. It had the slight drawback that it might make kids sick up their sandwiches and possibly take your picnic party for a plunge over a cliff.

4 FALSE – but a 1952 gadget featured a WASHING MACHINE strapped to a car's wheel. The problem was that if you went at more than 40 km per hour your clothes would be spun to shreds.

5 TRUE – believe it or not, in 2004 scientists at car-maker Toyota invented a computer-controlled car that narrowed its headlights when it was upset and raised "eyebrows" when surprised. When it was really upset it even shed tears but it didn't say rude words to traffic wardens.

6 TRUE – in 2005 a pair of British inventors drove to Italy in a car with an on-board toilet. In fact it's not a new idea – back in the 1900s a US millionaire ordered a luxury limo with a loo. He must have been flush with cash.

ER... DO YOU HAVE ANY TISSUE, DRIVER?

OF COURSE – THIS IS A **TOILET-ROLLS** ROYCE!

But car inventions aren't all fun and games. Every year, thousands of people were killed in car accidents. By 1951 over one million had died on the roads – and that was just in the USA. And cars parp out nasty gases too. Despite catalytic converters, cars produce a choking cocktail of grisly gases including carbon dioxide. Many scientists blame this gas for helping to warm the climate and causing extreme weather such as deadly droughts, horrible heatwaves and fatal floods.

BET YOU NEVER KNEW!

Most internal-combustion engines run on petrol or diesel fuel, but in 2005 a German inventor mixed a fuel made from 20 run-over dead cats and rotting rubbish.

WOW, IT GOES LIKE **STINK!**

Mind you, things were even worse back in the twentieth century when car exhaust gases contained lead too. In 1921 a chemical containing this poisonous metal was added to fuel to stop engines "knocking" – that's when the fuel doesn't burn properly. Before it was banned in the 1980s, the lethal lead damaged the brains of millions of people. As luck would have it the inventor is about to appear on the TV show where the guests are departed before they arrived…

DEAD BRAINY

THE SHOW FOR DEAD PEOPLE!

This week we've dug up Thomas Midgley (1889–1944) the US inventor who added a lead chemical to petrol.

Howdy!

RIP THOMAS MIDGLEY 1889

You made your discovery in 1921, and to show it was safe you breathed its stink for one minute...

Yes, I scented success.

It was a pity that the toxic chemical gave you lead poisoning.

GRURK!

NEW ICE-O-MATIC!

In 1930 you created a gas that you called "freon" for cooling fridges.

And I breathed it to show it was safe.

128

CONTINUED

So what do you think of cars now, readers? Well, I guess one thing's for sure. Some inventions can have evil effects even if the inventor meant to do good. After all, Thomas Midgley wanted to replace the poisonous gas used in fridges that sometimes leaked and killed people in their sleep.

Mind you, any fridge – and not just the poisoning ones – wouldn't get too cold without the power to make the chemicals inside them circulate through pipes and draw heat out of the fridge. But what is this useful and very helpful power? Well, the next chapter might come as a shock...

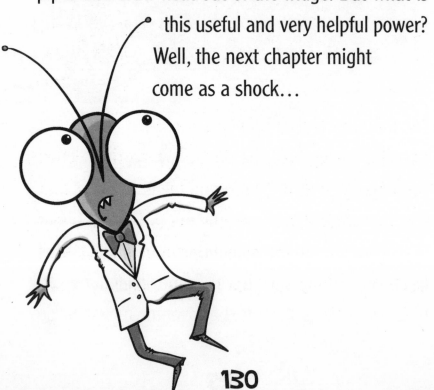

EXTREME ELECTRICAL INVENTIONS

This chapter is about…

TRINGGG! TRINGGG!

ER, 'SCUSE ME

Ten minutes later…

Isn't it amazing how the phone always rings when you're busy or at the wrong moment. Anyway, that was the editor and she wants me to tell you about the invention of the telephone and how it uses electricity to help you chat to your friends.

THE FULL PHONE STORY

Mind you, the first invention to use electricity to send messages wasn't the phone – it was the telegraph. It was invented in the 1830s and it worked by firing electrical pulses along a wire. The pulses took the form of Morse code – named after its US inventor Samuel Morse (1791–1872).

DARE YOU DISCOVER ... HOW TO MAKE MORSE CODE?

You will need:

• Two people (one can be you and the other needs to be a good friend). Make sure you both have fingernails.

• Two copies of this book – if you've only got one copy, you'll have to copy the next page.

- A couple of tables or school desks
- Paper and pencils

What you do:

1 Write a short message to send to your friend.

MR STINKS SMELLS

2 Using the code book, turn it into dots and dashes.

THE CODE BOOK

A ·–	H ····	O –––	V ···–
B –···	I ··	P ·––·	W ·––
C –·–·	J ·–––	Q ––·–	X –··–
D –··	K –·–	R ·–·	Y –·––
E ·	L ·–··	S ···	Z ––··
F ··–·	M ––	T –	
G ––·	N –·	U ··–	

3 Tap it out on the table top. You can tap the message with your fingernail for a dot and the soft part of your fingertip for a dash.

4 Your friend has to write down the dots and dashes and work out what they mean using the code book.

TERRIBLE TEACHER WARNING!

Beware! Some elderly teachers learnt Morse code way back in the mists of time. If you're caught sending a rude message you should blame it on your good friend and not me – right?

--. .-. .--. !!

BET YOU NEVER KNEW!

In 1845 the telegraph chalked up a first. In Britain it was used to catch a murderer. John Tawell killed his girlfriend and fled on the train from Slough. A quick-witted telegraph operator sent a description of the killer by telegraph to London and the police were waiting to trap tough-guy Tawell.

The telegraph proved a Victorian hit and its wires began to cross oceans, taking with them news stories and gossip. In fact, some people even got married by telegraph. But inventors were already hard at work on ideas to use electricity to carry speech along a wire…

The first to patent such an invention was Scottish-born American Alexander Graham Bell (1847–1922) in 1876, but lots of other inventors claimed to have beaten Bell to the bell. One of them, German science teacher Johann Philipp Reis, built a phone system at his school in 1861 using corks, knitting needles and sausage

135

skins. The only trouble was that it didn't work too well. Foiled Phil lost a court battle over who invented the phone first and I guess that he came out with a few crossed lines and felt a bit hung up about it…

We decided to ring Professor Z to ask him how Bell's phone worked…

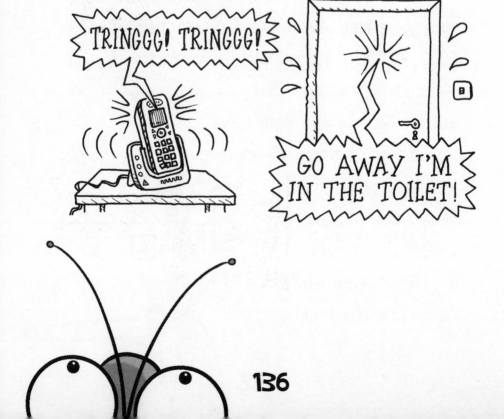

The phone used diaphragms* to turn sounds into vibrations that got passed to an electrically powered magnet where they made waves in the electrical current in the wire. At the other end the waves moved another magnet that vibrated another diaphragm and recreated the original sounds.

MAGNET

* Remember that word from page 54?

FLUSHHHHH!

GRR — I KNEW THAT!

A few years after he invented the telephone, Alexander Graham Bell came up with another shocking electric invention – a metal detector to find a bullet in a President's body. Here's what the medical reports might have looked like…

Medical Report on President Garfield
By Dr DW Bliss

3 July 1881
Yesterday a man shot President Garfield at the station here at Washington. The first doctor on the scene gave the President some medicine to relax him. The President sicked it up. Then I arrived and tried to remove the bullet from the President using a metal probe. The probe got stuck inside the President and he suffered extreme pain. I decided to use my fingers but that didn't work either.

26 July
The President is dying ... very slowly and painfully. His wound drips pus – I can't understand why it's got so bad. Today an inventor, Alexander Graham Bell, brought a machine designed to locate the bullet. It consists of a coil of wire linked to a battery and a second coil linked to one of Bell's new-fangled telephones. The idea is that if the first coil is near metal a faint hum will be picked up by the telephone.

Well, the machine worked – in a way. Bell heard humming all the time but he couldn't tell us where the bullet was. Meanwhile the poor President was petrified of getting an electric shock and I'm sure he never understood Bell's scientific gobbledegook. Bell says he can't understand it – the machine worked in the lab and found bullets hidden in his mouth and armpits. But not here. If you ask me all this modern technology is useless. There's no substitute for good old-fashioned fingers!

Actually the machine worked fine. It had simply detected the springs in the President's bed. Meanwhile 16 doctors battled to save the President, and most of them stuck their grubby fingers oozing with germs into his wound. On 19 September President Garfield died, killed as much by his doctors as by the bullet. That's what the gunman, Charles Guiteau, claimed at his trial. But the court didn't believe him and guilty Guiteau was executed anyway.

MEANWHILE BACK IN PROFESSOR Z'S SECRET HQ

Professor Z is just about to shrink Badog to the size of a pea and shove him in the toaster to show us how electricity can make a hot dog.

Electricity is made by particles called electrons that are even smaller than an atom. An electric current is made up of electrons moving in a wire.

1 Professor Z switches on the toaster to form an electric current in the wire. The electrons heat up the wire by friction.

2 The heat toasts the bread.

SWEAT!

3 Badog's getting hot under the collar too.

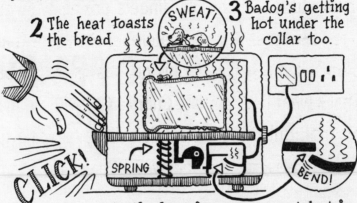

CLICK!

SPRING

BEND!

4 As the heat increases a metal strip swells and this makes it bend.

5 When it's hot enough the strip forms part of an electric circuit (the route for an electric current). This releases a catch, which releases a spring, and the toast pops up.

HOT TOAST

GDOING!

HOT DOG

CLICK!

141

HORRIBLE HEALTH WARNING!

Hopefully this fact should put you off trying any evil experiments involving mains electricity or taking electrical equipment to bits!

EXCITING ELECTRICITY TODAY

Today, most houses are overflowing with electric inventions. We decided to visit Professor Z's top-secret HQ to check out a few of them...

1 Vacuum cleaner (judging by the state of the HQ, it's not used too often). Hubert Cecil Booth invented the cleaner in 1901 after early cleaners blew dust rather than sucked it up. Another early pioneer, James Murray Spangler, built a cleaner in 1907 from an old box, a pillow slip, a fan, a broom handle, a stove pipe and a roller with goat's bristles stuck to it. And what's more, it worked!

2 Electric iron (never used by the look of the Prof's crumpled clothes). US inventor Henry W Seely came up with the electric iron in 1882. It was a great idea apart from the fact that hardly anyone had electric power at the time.

3 Electric torch (handy when the power fails). Conrad Hubert introduced the torch to America in the 1900s. Before then he sold a range of electric-bulb products including glow-in-the-dark skulls and scary faces to fix in a man's tie.

4 Electric washing machine (useful for removing bloodstains from lab coats). Washing machines were another US invention, developed in the 1900s. Mind you, all they did was stir your washing a bit and you had to do everything else by hand…

BET YOU NEVER KNEW!

In 1995 a washing machine seems to have inspired a surfing machine. This US invention featured a giant spinning drum of water, and all you had to was climb inside – and surf! That's if you didn't break every bone in your body first. Although this invention was patented it never got any further.

But talking about silly electrical inventions that were patented but never made it to the shops, here's a queasy quiz to test your inventive powers. You need to match each invention to its job, but to make the quiz harder, I've muddled up all the possible jobs and there are two spare…

144

THE WACKY "WHAT'S IT FOR?" QUIZ

FAILED INVENTION

1 A cone that goes round and round (USA 1999).
2 Lights around the toilet rim (USA 1993).
3 An electric pavement (USA 1909).
4 A battery in a walking stick (USA 1978).
5 An electrically wired classroom (Russia 1975).

POSSIBLE JOB

a) To suck up dog poo.
b) To pick up litter by magnetism.
c) To help old folk walk at 20 km per hour.
d) To give dogs an electric shock.
e) To give children electric shocks.
f) To guide you at night.
g) To make it easier to lick an ice cream.

1g) You can lick your ice cream into interesting sculptures.

2f) There were also lights set in the toilet floor like a kind of landing strip. The idea was to save turning on the light at night and you can even use it in the "wee" small hours. By the way, in the 1960s a Japanese inventor created a musical toilet. You had a choice of lively pop or relaxing classical melodies for those long sit-down sessions.

TOP OF THE PLOPS

TOP OF THE → POPS

3d) A stream of dog's wee can complete a circuit and give Badog a lesson he won't forget.

4a) The walking stick contained a bag that you could use ten times. A similar German invention sucked poo from the dog's body but I'm not going into any disgusting details!

5e) This evil invention aimed to make children learn by punishing them with electric shocks if they got the answers wrong. It actually worked but it's since been banned for cruelty so don't tell your evil teacher about it. She might try to un-ban it…

Wow – it looks like electrically powered inventions can do just about *anything*! In fact, did you know that in 1927 a British inventor even designed a machine to turn the pages of a book? Actually it only half-turned pages, but fortunately you've got some page-turning equipment of your own (they're on the ends of your hands). Hey – why not use them to turn the pages and inspect a few more awful adverts?

AWFUL ADVERTISEMENTS 3

There are loads of idiotic inventions aimed at improving your life, and some are meant to save your life (if they don't kill you first!). Hmm maybe it's a good thing these inventions failed to catch on and you can't buy them today...

ENJOY THE TIME OF YOUR LIFE

(while you still can!) Buy the...

TICK TICK *TICK TICK*

LIFE COUNTER WATCH

...it tells you how much longer you've got to live!

Simply program your wonderful watch with your lifestyle details. (BEWARE – if you smoke your life will be shorter!)
You'll see how much time you've got left to enjoy in years,

I'M A SKY-DIVING, TIGHT-ROPE WALKING, LION-TAMING, BOXER...

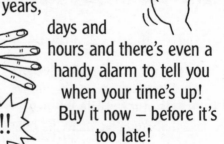

days and hours and there's even a handy alarm to tell you when your time's up! Buy it now – before it's too late!

ONE HOUR?!!!!

TAKE YOUR TIME ON THE TOILET!

(USA 1993)

This loo seat and clock makes an ideal gift for anyone with time on their hands (now they can have it under their backside too!).

➤ Spend all day with your bottom glued to the loo seat and find out how much time you've been wasting!

➤ Liven up Sunday mornings with a family "who can use the loo longest?" competition!

TICK TOCK
TICK TOCK
TICK TOCK
PLOP!

TAKE THE PAIN OUT OF INJECTIONS WITH THE
PINK BUNNY SYRINGE

(USA 1967)

Little kids hate having injections but they'll soon see the funny side of them with this new invention. You give them the bunny to play with and it suddenly stabs them with the needle.

THE SMALL PRINT
It's sure to give little kids a lifelong fear of rabbits.

OUCH!
NAUGHTY BUNNY!

149

ARE YOU TRAPPED IN A BURNING BUILDING?

Don't breathe the dangerous smoke! Be a survivor with the toilet snorkel (USA 1982). You stick the tube down the toilet and take a deep breath of the lovely healthy sewer gases!

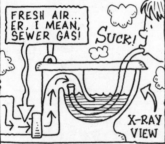

FRESH AIR... ER, I MEAN, SEWER GAS!

SUCK!

X-RAY VIEW

THE SMALL PRINT
Sewer gases can be as deadly as the smoke so DON'T TRY THIS AT HOME!

Finding it hard to get up in the morning? You need a blast from the

COLD AIR ALARM CLOCK

DRINGGGGGG!

VOOOSH!

AIR PUMP AND HOSE BLAST ICY AIR FROM YOUR AIR-CONDITIONING ON TO YOUR FACE

THE SMALL PRINT
1. This 1976 Canadian invention was obviously inspired by heartless parents who open children's bedroom windows on freezing school mornings.
2. The cold may cause your muscles to lock stiff so you can't get out of bed.

BEE SAFE ON THE MOVE! (USA 1996)

If you get attacked by a swarm of killer bees simply zip yourself up in this bag that looks like a coffin. You're sure to get a buzz, and if the bees get into your "bee safe" at least it will double as a real coffin!

BUZZ OFF!

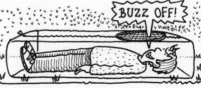

IF YOU CAN'T STAND THE HEAT GET OUT OF THE ... 5TH FLOOR!

You can still escape from a fire with this parachute hat and boots kit (USA 1879).

EH?

THE SMALL PRINT

1 The parachute is too small to be useful and the 5th floor is too low to parachute safely.

2 The sudden tug on your neck might pull your head off. And it's not a good idea to lose your head in an emergency!

IS BAD BREATH RUINING YOUR LIFE?

(USA 1990)

Simply strap on this attractive bad-breath face mask and you'll have to breathe out through your nose. You'll find out if your breath smells before your friends get round to telling you...!

URGH!

THE SMALL PRINT

You may look as if you've escaped from a high-security prison.

And now back to *Evil Inventions* where there's about to be something good on the telly AND the radio. Well, the next chapter is all about the telly and radio and it's really good!

Ready to tune in?

ROTTEN RADIO AND TERRIBLE TV

The first person to tune into radio waves was brilliant boffin Heinrich Hertz, but the radio we listen to today was the work of incredible inventor Guglielmo Marconi, and in 1901 he tried an amazing experiment – to send a radio signal across the Atlantic. But was it even *possible*?

153

NEWFOUNDLAND, 12 DECEMBER 1901

The young inventor scarcely noticed the howling wind that buffeted the walls and shook the rickety windows of his shack. He was busy listening to the hisses and crackles in his earphones, straining his ears for three tiny dots of sound. A ghostly signal flying through the stormy air from a distant coast 4,800 km away.

But would he hear anything?

Experts and scientists said "NO". They thought the experiment wouldn't work. And if they were right would anyone ever take Marconi seriously again?

Then suddenly he heard something.

Three clicks.

"Can you hear anything, Mr Kemp?" he asked his engineer excitedly.

George Kemp took the earphones and frowned. To Marconi's relief, he heard the clicks too. They were the Morse-code signal for "S" and they had been sent from the coast of England, flying at 300,000 km a second over the stormy ocean to be picked up by Marconi's aerial. The aerial was flying from a kite that was just now in danger of blowing away. Marconi smiled quietly to himself. He knew he had been right all along…

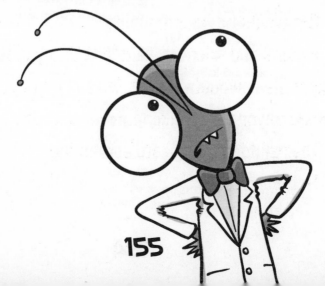

INCREDIBLE INVENTOR FILES

NAME: Guglielmo Marconi (1874–1937)

NATIONALITY: Italian

CLAIM TO FAME: Guglielmo believed that radio had a BIG future as a new kind of communication that could span the world. No one in Italy took him seriously, but he moved to Britain and made his dream come true.

INCREDIBLE INVENTIONS: Every year he made his radio sets and aerials more powerful until he could send messages across oceans.

DREADFUL DETAILS: In 1912 the Titanic, the world's biggest ship, hit an iceberg and started to sink. Radio operator Jack Phillips used one of Marconi's radio sets to send out a plea for help. Jack died in the disaster, but as a result of his bravery 705 people were rescued.

DON'T MENTION: In 1912 Marconi was accused of secret deals with the British government to set up radio stations.
Talk and music radio. Marconi didn't like the idea – he thought radio should stick to Morse code. He was wrong.

AWFUL END: Marconi was right to imagine that radio could be a worldwide industry. When he died in 1937 every radio station on Earth went silent for two minutes in memory of a great scientist and a great inventor.

A SIGNAL OF RESPECT

SILENCE!

Well, that's the story of how radio started, but now for a question you've probably never asked yourself as you listen. How does your radio actually work? Well, the signal that brings your favourite radio show is carried by radio waves and that's where I get stuck, er, ... Professor Z, so what are radio waves?

157

Radio waves are waves of electromagnetic* energy made by atoms.

 HUH?

HORRIBLE SCIENCE WARNING!

COMPLICATED SCIENCE AHEAD — you may have to read this bit very slowly!

The closer together the tops of the radio waves are, the higher the frequency of the wave.

In a radio station a microphone turns sounds into a varying electrical current. And then a transmitter turns the electrical current into radio waves.

RADIO STATION

HELLO!

TRANSMITTER

CARRIER WAVE

RADIO STATION

HELLO

TRANSMITTER

SOUND WAVES

The actual radio waves carrying the sounds are included in a radio wave with a special frequency called the carrier wave that the radio station broadcasts all the time.

*Electromagnetic means they're electric and magnetic.

When the radio waves hit the radio aerial they produce an electric current based on the voice-radio signals plus the carrier signal.

I tune the radio to get the carrier-signal frequency — in this case relaxing classical music.

SNATCH!

The electric current with the sound signal is made more powerful and the loudspeakers play the sounds.

SNATCH!

HERE'S JEZ LIZNIN PLAYING THE BLOODSUCKERS WITH EVIL ROCK!

TREMENDOUS TV

As soon as anyone invents anything there's always a queue of other inventors trying to improve it. Radio was a staggering success but by the 1920s inventors wanted to go one better — they wanted to broadcast pictures and invent TV. But as usual with inventing it's easier to hit on an idea than to make it work.

In fact the person to get there first was a scruffy, sickly inventor named John Logie Baird (1888–1946). Baird dedicated years of his life to this epic effort but his TV produced a terrible picture and it's not the TV technology we use today. We'll take a look at a modern TV later but before then did you know that the first face on TV belonged to a ventriloquist's dummy named Stooky Bill? We interviewed Bill to find out how Baird invented TV.

GOODBYE MAGAZINE

My life as a TV star by STOOKY BILL

With roving reporter Randall Scandal

Randall: Tell me about your memories of John Logie Baird.

Bill: I never had much time for Baird – he was a real dummy.

Randall: Like you, you mean?

Bill: Ha ha – very funny. Baird was a failed inventor. He invented a new type of shoes and fell over wearing a pair. He invented a rust-proof razor…

Randall: That sounds like the cutting edge of technology…

Bill: I should say so – Baird cut himself so badly he had to give up the idea. By the time I met him he had no money and was living in a poky attic. He looked half-crazed with his wild hair and staring eyes…

Randall: That does sound like you.

(At this point Bill stared at me in a very unnerving way.)

Randall: Tell me about your first TV appearance…

Bill: Baird's TV was a load of old rubbish. Well, that's what it was made of. It was just a hatbox lid with holes cut in it stuck on a darning needle and turned by a fan.

Randall: Who was this fan?

Bill: NOT A HUMAN FAN, YOU DUMMY – AN ELECTRIC FAN! In fact Baird didn't have any human fans. Everyone laughed at him because his TV didn't work. But he carried on tinkering until it did work. On 2 October he stuck me in front of the machine. I had to look at a set of light bulbs and I nearly cooked, but hey, I'm a professional so I didn't complain…

Randall: I bet Baird was happy when he saw a picture…

Bill: He was so excited that he dashed to an office downstairs and grabbed a boy named William Taynton. Baird stuck the lad in front of the machine and asked him to stick out his tongue and move his head.

"William, I've seen you, I've seen you!" shouted Baird. Well, he never sounded so pleased when he saw me. Then they swapped places.

Randall: I've heard Baird had to pay William to stay sweating in front of the hot bright machine.

Bill: Well, luvvie, to be frank, that's a bit of a sore point. You see *I've* never been paid. So what are you paying for this interview?

Randall (grabbing coat): Is that the time? Sorry – gotta dash – there's something good on the telly…

Baird had trouble seeing William's face because his picture was so terrible. The picture was made from light that passed through the holes in the spinning hatbox lid, but it must have been like trying to see through soup.

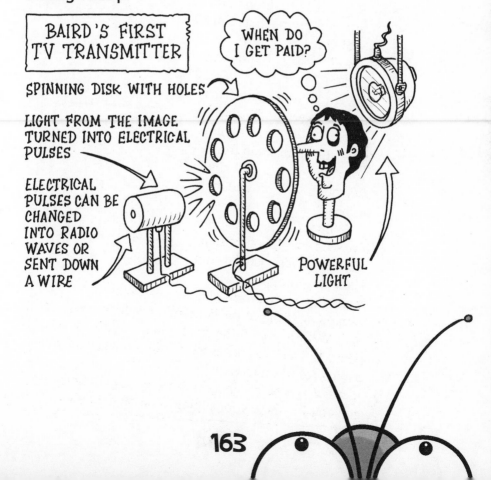

BAIRD'S FIRST
TV TRANSMITTER

WHEN DO
I GET PAID?

SPINNING DISK WITH HOLES

LIGHT FROM THE IMAGE
TURNED INTO ELECTRICAL
PULSES

ELECTRICAL
PULSES CAN BE
CHANGED
INTO RADIO
WAVES OR
SENT DOWN
A WIRE

POWERFUL
LIGHT

COULD YOU BE AN INVENTOR?

What did Baird use for a TV experiment?

a) A colour-blind hamster.
b) A high-flying kite.
c) A human eyeball.

ANSWER

Answer: c) Baird knew that eyeballs contain a light-sensitive substance (that's how we see) — so he decided to check it out. A friendly surgeon was just about to remove an eyeball at a local hospital and he offered it to the inventor. Baird took the revolting relic home wrapped in his hankie, but messed up his attempt to cut it up and had to throw it away.

Although Baird improved his TV picture, it remained terrible. When the BBC tested it in 1936 they weren't too impressed…

REPORT TO THE DIRECTOR GENERAL OF THE BBC
By Mike Gaffertape, Studio Manager

Baird's TV is TERRIBLE! His cameras are so noisy that we have to shut them in a soundproof room. And they're so dangerous we have to bolt them to the floor. The picture quality is awful – in order to be seen, the poor actors have to wear yellow make-up and blue lips and when their make-up melts under the hot studio lights they look like monsters. And anyone who wears red looks as if they're naked.

THIS IS THE NEWS

Meanwhile other inventors were working on a new TV system. The inventors were Vladimir Zworykin (1889–1982) and Philo Farnsworth

(1906–1971) in the USA, and a teacher named Kenjiro Takayanagi (1899–1990) in Japan. Working separately, each of the inventors came up with the idea of electronic TV – a better system than Baird's version. In 1937 the BBC scrapped Baird's TV and opted for electronic TV. Inside this new type of TV a beam of electrons zapped a screen. The screen was coated with a substance that produced light where the electrons hit it. The result was sharper, clearer pictures.

The first TVs cost a year's wages for a goldfish bowl-sized screen that you could only watch for two hours a day. But TV got better and by the 1960s millions of people were glued to the goggle-box. But how the heck did they work?

166

MEANWHILE BACK IN PROFESSOR Z'S TOP-SECRET HQ...

The evil inventor has shrunk Badog down to a tiny size so that he can explain the insides of his clapped-out old 1990s TV.

TV camera separates blue, green and red colours to make three electric signals.

The TV aerial picks up and sorts out the signals.

Microphone creates a sound signal

SEE ANYTHING, PROF?

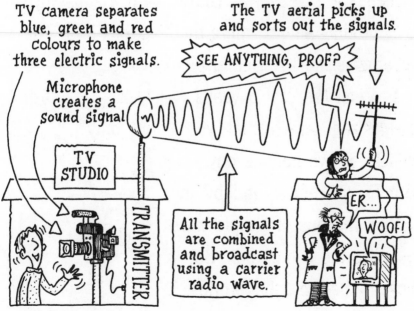

TV STUDIO

TRANSMITTER

All the signals are combined and broadcast using a carrier radio wave.

ER...

WOOF!

Actually the evil Prof's TV is out of date. Modern TV screens use LEDs to create brighter, sharper pictures. LEDs or as the boffins call them, light-emitting diodes, control the flow of electrons to produce light. You can find LEDs everywhere from traffic lights to digital alarm clocks. And modern TVs and radios tune into digital signals – I'll describe the digital details on page 182.

BRILLIANT BRAINWAVES

Radio and TV are incredible, aren't they? But they're not the only inventions that use waves of electromagnetic energy. Here are a few more that you might have heard of…

1 Radar uses radio waves in the same way as you use sounds to make echoes. An aerial sends out high-frequency radio waves and detects the radio-wave echoes bouncing off an object such as a plane. This brilliant brainwave was the work of scientist Robert Watson-Watt (1892–1973) in 1935, and in the Second World War radar warned Britain of German aircraft attacks. In 1954 Watson-Watt was in Canada when he was caught speeding in his car, by police using a radar gun. The scientist was on his way to give a speech … on radar.

2 The microwave oven was invented because one day in 1945 US inventor Percy Le Baron Spencer had an embarrassing accident. He was strolling past a magnetron (a device used in radar that produces microwaves) and a choccie bar turned to goo in his pocket. Puzzled Percy blew up popcorn and exploded an egg using microwaves and realized he'd hit on a new way to cook food. In fact microwaves zap atoms in water and heat them up – so I guess this was a real hot discovery...

3 Your TV remote control uses LEDs to make infrared rays. Infrared rays are electromagnetic waves that you feel as heat. But they're not harmful – so DON'T PANIC – you can't zap the cat or bake your butt by sitting on the remote!

4 A mobile phone is basically a portable radio transmitter – pioneered in the USA in the 1940s. The marvellous mobile can communicate with a local radio aerial, which is part of a mobile phone network.

Mind you, nowadays, mobiles are more than just phones. They've got digital cameras and internet connections – in fact they'll do everything except brush your teeth and do your homework. The secrets of all these inventions are found in the eye-popping world of computers and electronics in the next chapter. So are you ready to have your eyeballs popped?

CLEVER COMPUTERS

Where would we be without computers?

Well, children couldn't play computer games, the Internet would be a fishing net and this book would have been written with a scratchy old biro. But on the plus side, adults wouldn't get grumpy because their computer crashed...

NO THEY'D BE GRUMPY ABOUT SOMETHING ELSE!

HOW COMPUTERS BEGAN

People invented computers because they hated sums and needed machines to help with the mind-numbing maths. First came the abacus invented in Iraq before 300 BC. It's still in use in China and Japan, and trained operators can be as fast as a pocket calculator. Now there's a machine you can really count on!

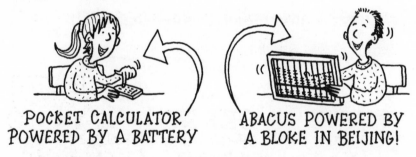

POCKET CALCULATOR POWERED BY A BATTERY

ABACUS POWERED BY A BLOKE IN BEIJING!

In the 17th century, inventors such as Frenchman Blaise Pascal (1623–1662) and German Wilhelm Schickard (1592–1635) built calculating machines. But Victorian inventors such as Charles Babbage

(1791–1871) dreamt of creating even more powerful calculating machines. Brilliant Babbage talked the British government into handing over thousands of pounds to build a machine that he never finished. You may like to know that in 1991, experts at the Science Museum built a part of the planned machine and it worked! In 2012 it was on display close to Babbage's pickled brainy brain (and no, I don't know what it was doing there – just chilling out, I guess).

Babbage's machine wasn't electric for the very good reason that there was no electric power yet. But later inventors worked on electric computers, including German Konrad Zuse (1910–1995) (who built one in his parents' living room), American Vannevar Bush and Briton Alan Turing (1912–1954).

During the Second World War talented Turing worked at the top-secret British code-breaking HQ that cracked the fiendishly hard German codes. And he worked on early computers that cracked the codes faster and according to some experts shortened the war by a year and saved millions of lives. After the war Turing built new computers, but he suffered personal problems and became more and more depressed. At last the incredible inventor took his own life by eating a poisoned apple. He was only 42.

Early computers were like dinosaurs – that's to say they were huge and dangerous and stupid. In fact even the most powerful early computers had less brainpower than a pocket calculator. At first they used devices called valves to control the electric current. The valves looked like light bulbs and used huge amounts of electricity. They were so hot that the computers needed air conditioning to work at all.

Of course computers aren't like that today (if they were your school's electrics would blow up every time someone played a computer game). And the reason why today's computers are smaller and faster and more powerful is all to do with chips...

WANT ONE?

NO, MICROCHIPS, SILLY!

MAGNIFICENT MICROCHIPS

1 A microchip is the most jaw-dropping, dribble-dripping invention ever. Imagine a city with all its roads and buildings shrunk down to the size of your little fingernail. Well, that's a microchip, but instead of being a city of little people and cars and dogs it's a city of electrons built on a sliver of silicon mixed with other chemicals (silicon is a substance found in sand).

2 The microchip was invented in 1958 by Americans Robert Noyce and Jack Kilby (working separately). Jack had just started working for electronics company Texas Instruments. One day the firm closed for a holiday but as a new employee, Jack had to stay at work. It was then that he had his great idea – so I suppose you can say "all work and no play DOESN'T make Jack a dull boy!"

3 Each microchip contains hundreds of parts such as transistors. These are tiny switches that go on and off to produce pulses of electrical current, which can be used to make commands or store information.

BET YOU NEVER KNEW!

In 2001 scientists at Tokyo University wired a microchip to a cockroach's nerves. The scientists used a remote control zapper to make the bug scuttle in different directions. "What next?" I hear you gasp. "The robot little brother?"

BAFFLING BINARY CODE

Although different computers can be programmed using different codes known as "languages", every language is based ultimately on binary code. It's a number system in which a number is written as 1s or 0s. In a computer, letters or commands are turned into binary numbers where 1 is an on electric current and 0 is off. It's a bit like you trying to send a coded message by switching a light on or off. Just think – your favourite computer games, digital photos, DVDs and even the toilet timer on page 149, all depend on tiny on-off electric pulses!

Anyway, let's see how Professor Z's evil computer works.

NICE TAIL, MATE!

1 The keyboard sends info to the computer. The keyboard turns letters that you type into binary code.

2 The mouse allows you to control a cursor on the screen. As you move the mouse a roller turns wheels. Light shines through slots in the wheels and turns into a pattern of on-off light pulses that get turned into binary code.

3 The screen displays information.

4 Inside the computer there are different chips with different jobs – for example memory chips store info in the form of electric pulses.

COMPUTERS TAKE OVER THE WORLD

Each year computers grow faster and more powerful thanks to more complex microchips. And each year there are more and more computer-controlled inventions. For example, they control robot probes on other planets and even high-tech anti-snoring beds. It's true – in 2004 Swedish scientists invented the world's first computerized anti-snoring bed that stops your dad snoring by propping him up so that his tongue doesn't cover his throat.

Mind you that's just a teeny taster of what computer technology can do – take TV for example. Today's digital TVs are a world away from the fuzzy old flicker boxes that your granny used to be glued to. A digital TV decodes a signal sent in binary code. The signal has been treated using clever technology developed for computers called compression. This strips out some of the signal – although not enough for you to notice – and allows more info to be sent.

More info means that the signal provides bigger and more detailed pictures. And loads more channels to choose from. What's that? You're bored of digital TV already? Oh well, you could always tune in to digital radio which uses the same technology to bring you loads more ultra-clear radio stations. Or you could play a computer game. You could play with your good friend from page 132 (if you're still talking, that is)...

OH, GO ON THEN!

COMPUTERS GET COOL

Experts can't agree who invented computer games but US scientist Willy Higinbotham devised one of the first in 1958. Willy created the bouncing ball screen game to play at his lab open day. Amazingly, hundreds of people queued to play this silly game – well, no one had ever seen anything like it. Years later Willy's kids asked him why he hadn't made a fortune from the game. The scientist shrugged and said he hadn't realized he could patent the idea. Oh well, you win some...

In the 1960s, the US Department of Defence planned to link computers in a network. They hoped that in a war fought with atom bombs, at least some computers would survive and stay in touch. Then Paul Baran in the USA and Donald Davies in Britain invented a system that allowed computers to send messages to each other along phone lines. It was the start of something BIG – today we call it the Internet and email.

The Internet	
1969	**4 computers**
1971	**23 computers**
1998	**130 million computers**
Today	**BILLIONS of computers**

In 1989 a scientist, Tim Berners-Lee, invented the worldwide web – a kind of address system to find and open documents on the Internet. Within twenty years, thanks to the worldwide web, the Internet took over the world. People used it for shopping and ordering pizzas and watching films and chatting with their friends on social media sites and playing games online. Meanwhile there were websites for just about everything including Horrible

Science! In 2013 scientists were even experimenting with sending tastes over the Internet using a device to give the tongue electric shocks. Just think – one day you could watch an Internet movie and taste it too. Let's hope it's not a horror film about eating worms and rotten cabbage!

And that's not all. Thanks to the 3D printer, developed by inventor Chuck Hull in 1984, it's possible to send instructions to make things over the Internet. Guided by a computer and using a computer model, the printer builds an object, layer by layer, in front of your eyes. A 3D printer can make just about anything, and in 2013 scientists were even experimenting with making artificial body bits. Would you fancy printing a spare liver in your living-room?

The 3D printer is definitely not the only Internet-linked gadget. There are thousands of them! How about a cat collar that you use to track your cat online? Or a toaster that tells you the weather – it's true!

BET YOU NEVER KNEW!

In 2001 a British scientist invented an Internet-linked toaster that could burn an image of the day's weather – sun, cloud or rain on your toast. Can you imagine how this invention might have developed? The toaster could have made soggy toast when it was going to rain and frozen toast when it was going to snow!

WHAT'S THE WEATHER FORECAST, DEAR?

SLURP!

SCORCHING!

Talking about really chilly food, did you know that in the 1990's a Swedish company invented the world's first computerized intelligent *fridge*.

What a cool invention (groan!). But hold on a minute – isn't it just a teeny-weeny bit scary when your fridge has a better brain than your little sister? Oh well, at least the fridge is designed to make life easier. The invention in the next chapter was designed to kill people and destroy cities – now that really was scary...

THE ATOM BOMB

Remember how Archimedes came up with war machines to defend his city from the Romans?

In wartime, inventors often work on deadly inventions. In the Second World War, inventors were at the front of the struggle, designing bigger bombs, more powerful planes and terrible tanks. And in America an international team of scientists set to work on the most destructive weapon ever. They thought they were doing the world a favour. But before I tell you what happened there's a few science words I ought to explain…

1 The centre of an atom is made of small particles called **neutrons** and **protons**

2 Heavier types of atom such as **uranium** and **plutonium** have lots of them (that's why they're heavier).

3 These substances are dangerously **radioactive** — that is, they spit out **neutrons** that can harm people.

EINSTEIN'S WARNING

Long Island, USA – 19 July 1939

The two men were hot and tired. They had driven for hours and now they were hopelessly lost.

"Let's give up and go home – perhaps fate intended it," said Leo Szilard to the driver of the car, Eugene Wigner.

"No, let's ask a child," said Eugene. "After all, every child knows him."

As luck would have it soon afterwards they spotted a small boy standing by the road clutching a fishing rod.

"Do you know where Albert Einstein lives?" asked Leo.

"Of course I do," replied the boy. And he pointed the two men in the right direction.

"See what I mean?" said Eugene as they drove off.

I guess that's why we're here, thought Leo. *To make sure there's a future for kids like him.*

The two men were scientists and they were both desperately worried. They believed that the future of the world depended on what they did next.

Back in 1933, Leo Szilard realized that you could split radioactive atoms by firing neutrons at them but if the process went out of control it would cause an enormous explosion. It was called a chain reaction. Recently German scientists Otto Hahn and Fritz Strassmann had created the start of a chain reaction.

Szilard and Wigner were Hungarian Jews. They had been forced to leave their homes by supporters of the German Nazi Party who hated Jews. Now they were terrified that Germany might use the discovery to build a new kind of bomb – an atom bomb that could destroy a city. If the Nazis built the bomb they could conquer the world.

At last the scientists pulled up in a cloud of dust outside a small shabby cabin and an old man came out to see who they were. He had wild white hair and he was dressed in shorts and sandals. At last they had found him – Albert Einstein – the most famous scientist in the world. Both scientists knew Einstein well, he had been their teacher. A few years after that Szilard had worked with the great scientist on designs for a new type of fridge.

Over tea in the shady porch of the cabin, Einstein listened quietly as Leo and Eugene told him about the danger of a Nazi bomb. He was amazed because he had been too busy with his own work to keep up with the latest  discoveries. Then he bowed his head and said: "I hadn't thought of that."

Einstein felt deeply shocked. He hated war, and although he was a German he had refused to support his country in the First World War. But like his visitors that day, Einstein was Jewish and he too had been forced to flee to America.

The scientists decided to warn the President of

the United States about the danger and Szilard wrote and Einstein signed a letter. Alerted by the letter, President Roosevelt set up the most gigantic weapons project in history. Szilard and Wigner worked on the project but Einstein was banned for political reasons.

Eighteen months later the scientists managed to create a chain reaction. But Szilard felt sad.

"This day will go down as a black day in the history of mankind," he remarked.

Szilard was having doubts about the bomb and soon afterwards he dropped out after arguments with General Groves, the soldier in charge of the project. Meanwhile the scientists built two types of bomb. One based on uranium and the other on plutonium.

By this time, Germany had been defeated and the scientists knew the truth. There was no Nazi atom bomb. The German scientists didn't even know how to make one. But the USA and Japan were at war. Desperately, Leo Szilard pleaded with the new President, Harry Truman, not to use the bomb. But the President wouldn't listen. He gave the order to drop the bomb on Japan.

The 6 August was a beautiful morning. At about 8.15 a plane called the *Enola Gay* dropped a uranium  bomb on the city of Hiroshima. Within minutes, the city with its quarter of a million people had ceased to exist. All that was left were burning ruins and blasted, blinded survivors crawling about with terrible wounds. Three days later a plutonium bomb destroyed the city of Nagasaki. Japan surrendered.

Many people outside Japan welcomed the dropping of the atom bomb. They thought that by ending the war it actually prevented far worse suffering. But not everyone agreed. When someone told Einstein the news of Hiroshima he put his head in his hands and said simply, "Oh why?!"

The gentle old scientist blamed himself for the atomic bombing. Later he said that if he had known what was to happen he would have become a watchmaker. You might think that the atom bomb sounds horribly scary – and you'd be right. But that's not the end of the story. Just as shared danger can bring people together – so the threat of a war fought with atom bombs has brought out the best in some people.

BET YOU NEVER KNEW!

Leo Szilard wasn't the only scientist to quit the atom bomb project. Polish-born Joseph Rotblat walked out too. After 1945 the USA and Russia developed even more destructive bombs and built so many that eventually they had the power to destroy all human life. But Joseph dedicated the rest of his life to bringing scientists from both sides together to warn of the dangers of war. In 1998 after 50 years of devoted effort Joseph Rotblat received his rightful reward – the Nobel Prize. It was for Peace.

Today, thanks in part to the protests of people all over the world, there are agreements designed to limit the spread of destructive weapons. They're still there, of course, but at least people are trying to control them.

EPILOGUE: NOT-SO-EVIL INVENTIONS

This book is called *Evil Inventions* and some inventions were meant to have evil effects on people. There were machines to torture and kill and weapons of war. Other inventions had bad effects that their inventors never intended – just think of poor Thomas Midgley and his gruesome gases.

But most inventions aren't like that. I mean you can't call bicycles or TVs or computers "evil"… Well, I suppose your parents might be in an evil mood if you cycled over their flower beds, and spent the rest of the day watching TV and playing computer games. But that doesn't make these inventions evil.

And some inventions have done a lot of good. Just think of lifesaving lighthouses, for example, or seat belts. In 1958 Swedish inventor Nils Ivar Bohlin (1920–2002) designed a seat belt that fitted diagonally across the body. Earlier seat belts secured the waist and it was terribly easy for a person's head to smash against the windscreen in a crash. Nils' invention was safer and more comfortable than the old seat belts, and the Volvo car company sold it without a patent so that anyone could copy the idea. Today every car in the world has one of Nils' seat belts and they've saved countless lives. Nils Bohlin said:

Sometimes I get a call from some grateful person who has survived thanks to my belt. It warms my heart and shows that I have been able to do something for mankind.

What better reason is there to invent anything? But that's the whole point. In the end any invention is no more evil or good than the purpose we use it for. And that's our choice. Happy Horrible Science, everyone!